ADDITIONAL PRAISE FOR
THE SONGWRITER'S HANDBOOK

"*The Songwriter's Handbook* is a witty, drole, yet informative tome rich with colorful anecdotes and important information for any aspiring songwriter. I highly recommend it." —**David Benoit**, GRAMMY-nominated pianist, composer, and arranger

"I greatly admire Mark Winkler's excellent songwriting skills—his understanding of the songwriting craft is second to none. In this book, he shares invaluable insights alongside his own personal experiences which are funny and poignant. This is such a valuable handbook for all up-and-coming songwriters everywhere, whatever their level of experience." —**Claire Martin**, OBE, jazz singer, three-time winner of the British Jazz Awards

"Mark Winkler lays out clearly and concisely the rules of the road for writing popular songs. He gives you the lay of the land and the map of the territory. Don't wait for the angel of inspiration to land on your pen—get down to work with *The Songwriter's Handbook* and get ready for the ride of a lifetime." —**Ben Sidran**, producer and keyboardist; host of NPR's Jazz Alive

"What a brilliant work on songwriting! The information on lyric writing is wonderfully detailed and on point. This well-researched book is full of insights that will help boost every artist's musicianship." —**John Clayton**, GRAMMY-winning bassist, composer, producer, and leader of the Clayton Hamilton Big Band

"Few creative endeavors are as challenging or as rewarding as crafting timeless lyrics. Mark Winkler's expertise—both as a respected songwriter and an uplifting mentor—is distilled into chapters rich in practical guidance, uplifting empathy, and a profound commitment to the power of the popular song." —**Dan Kimpel**, author, educator, and music journalist

"I had the opportunity to sit in on a Mark Winkler songwriting class many years ago and was delighted to see what a natural gift he had for teaching (as well as writing songs). I knew his book would be good, but I was blown away

by how comprehensive Mark's topic coverage and analysis are. Great job!"
—**Lorraine Feather**, singer, lyricist, and songwriter; three-time GRAMMY nominee and seven-time Emmy nominee

"Mark Winkler is top in his field, and his book is a reflection of his talent. It's fun to read and totally instructive at the same time. You will learn so much, and you will be smiling when you see how good your songs get! *The Songwriter's Handbook* will make a real difference in a lot of songwriter's lives." —**Allan Rich**, Oscar- and Golden Globe-nominated writer of songs for Whitney Houston, Natalie Cole, and Barbra Streisand

"Whether you want to write a song, sing a song, or even just appreciate music in a new and fascinating way, this is an amazingly entertaining book! Mark Winkler is a masterful teacher and an even more masterful storyteller."
—**Andrea Marcovicci**, Golden Globe-nominated singer and actress; inductee, Cabaret Hall of Fame

"Considering how personal and subjective songwriting can be, Mark Winkler skillfully and carefully distills the process into easy-to-understand (and apply!) step-by-step suggestions allowing for individuality. The tone of each chapter fosters camaraderie, encouragement, and guidance." —**Rene Marie**, GRAMMY-nominated songwriter and jazz singer

"Mark Winkler is a gifted—not to mention prolific—lyricist who really knows his stuff. If you have an interest in good lyric writing, or just insightful showbiz stories, then you need to get this book!" —**Grant Geissman**, GRAMMY- and Emmy-nominated guitarist/composer

"One of the most educational, insightful, and complete books on songwriting I've ever read. It's not only a primer on how to craft great songs, but a meticulous map on how to navigate the often murky, and always turbulent, waters of professional songwriting." —**Phil Swann**, songwriter and author

THE SONGWRITER'S HANDBOOK

THE SONGWRITER'S HANDBOOK

Power Strategies for Crafting Great Lyrics

MARK WINKLER

ROWMAN & LITTLEFIELD
Lanham • Boulder • New York • London

Edited by Ronny S. Schiff

Published by Rowman & Littlefield
An imprint of The Rowman & Littlefield Publishing Group, Inc.
4501 Forbes Boulevard, Suite 200, Lanham, Maryland 20706
www.rowman.com

86-90 Paul Street, London EC2A 4NE

Copyright © 2024 by Mark Winkler

All rights reserved. No part of this book may be reproduced in any form or by any electronic or mechanical means, including information storage and retrieval systems, without written permission from the publisher, except by a reviewer who may quote passages in a review.

British Library Cataloguing in Publication Information Available

Library of Congress Cataloging-in-Publication Data

ISBN 978-1-5381-8069-3 (cloth)
ISBN 978-1-5381-8070-9 (paper)
ISBN 978-1-5381-8071-6 (electronic)

This book is dedicated to my late husband of thirty-four years, Richard Del Belso. His constant love and support were just what this struggling artist needed. He was my best advisor, confidante, and critic. He opened my eyes to the world, and then I wrote what I saw.

CONTENTS

Foreword — xi
Preface — xiii

1. Introduction — 1
2. A Working Songwriter — 3
3. How to Judge If Your Lyric Is Good — 11
4. Come Up with a Great Title — 15
5. Song Forms — 23
6. Be Specific — 33
7. Top Ten Tips for Lyric Writers: Tips 1–5 — 39
8. Rewriting the Beatles, and Other Things — 43
9. Rhyming — 53
10. Laundry List Songs — 61
11. Top Ten Tips for Lyric Writers: Tips 6–10 — 67
12. Tropical Nights: Me 'n' Liza! — 77
13. Getting Outside Your Bubble — 87
14. Writing to an Existing Melody — 95
15. Performing Live — 103

16	Break Time!	113
17	Writing for the Musical Theater	117
18	Strategies for Creating New Songs	131
19	Show, Don't Tell	143
20	Write a Song Like a Movie	151
21	Writing with Collaborators	161
22	Dirty Little Secrets of Songwriting	167
23	Am I Doing This Thing Right?	179
24	You Can Write a Song	185
25	A Song Is Like a House	195
26	Publishing and Copyrighting	197
27	Final Review	207
28	What Do I Do Now?	213

Glossary	225
Song Lyrics Permissions	233
Index	237
Song Index	245
About the Author	249

FOREWORD

I admire the way Mark Winkler tells things like he sees them. And because he sees with such clarity, he tells in memorable detail. So, when Mark Winkler tells us how to write the lyrics to a song, we start to see, clearly, how we can do it. Through precise examples and detailed exercises, Mark makes something as magical and mysterious as songwriting into something actionable and doable, without robbing the process of that magic.

"Specificity gives your song authenticity!" Mark tells his students with conviction. I love how he is at once catchy and instructive by example. Well-chosen details, he teaches us, evoke emotion. They make the song feel personal and real. Mark provides numerous exercises to help us enact this and other valuable principles, authentically.

My favorite exercise in this book is one Mark has been assigning to his classes at The Songwriting School of Los Angeles for more than a decade, asking students both online and in-person to "Re-Write the Beatles." We take the classic song, "Penny Lane" and write our own version about a place specific to us—while precisely following the rhythm, rhyme, and form of the original. This yields far more than a simple parody.

As emerging songwriters, the process of inserting our life's details into the space where McCartney's have gone allows us to briefly step in the footprints of a master, matching our stride to his. We trace the rise and fall of stresses in the lines to learn their rhythms. We map the pattern of rhymes and go where they lead. We follow the path of an iconic song and learn to forge paths of our own.

Beyond the mechanics of how the lines move, we get marching orders for the sections themselves. The strategy of each line becomes an instruction manual for how to drive a lyric forward from start to end. With specific examples, detailed explanations, and exercises like this one, Mark makes something lofty feel attainable. He takes something elusive and moves it within reach.

In addition to teaching the craft of lyric writing, this book offers helpful professional advice as well. As a platinum lyricist with hundreds of cuts to his name and as a charting jazz recording artist, Mark acknowledges the people who steadfastly shepherded him along in his career. He urges aspiring songwriters to find respected "gatekeepers" of our own. No, not dear *mom*, who will tell us everything we do is genius (*thanks, mom . . .*). He means industry pros who know to call us out when the work is not there yet. The best gatekeepers don't just tell us we're not there—they point the way. In this book, Mark Winkler points the way with confidence and encouragement.

I have had the privilege of introducing Mark Winkler to countless enthusiastic workshops and classes at The Songwriting School over the past dozen-plus years, and I feel proud and honored to introduce him and this, his first book on the craft of songwriting, now. When I read these pages, I hear Mark's cheery, melodic voice in every line—irreverently funny, genuinely insightful, and generously kind. In them, he cites as examples the lyrics of many students from The Songwriting School and from his classes at UCLA Extension. His teaching pulls inspired work from his students. They adore him every bit as much as he loves songs and songwriters. His affection for the work and for those who do it comes through in each section of the book.

The Songwriter's Handbook is our guide for that important work. Let's get to it!

—Rob Seals
Founder and Director of The Songwriting School of Los Angeles
thesongwritingschool.com

PREFACE

One of the perks of teaching new students all the time is the wonderful discovery that each student has their own personal story to tell. And it's my job as an instructor to have them write that story in their own "voice"—and not in mine.

I've been wanting to write this book for a long time. While teaching lyric writing classes over the last twenty years, I had formulated a syllabus. Then through the different classes I've taught, I had refined and polished it and filled it in with stories, insights, and little nuggets of wisdom that would come up when working through the material. But it took the COVID-19 epidemic to give me the necessary time to sit down and do it—and a little bit of serendipity.

Heather Perram Frank contacted me about being a private student. She had been recommended by Chris Loudon, longtime jazz vocal critic for *Jazz Times* magazine. In the business, he was one of those people who "got" me and constantly supported my work through the years. So, when Heather mentioned she wanted to write songs, he suggested me with a strong recommendation. It turned out Heather had been an editor and worked with Chris on several magazines through the years. I gave her songwriting lessons, and she took to it like a literary duck to water—and she helped me shape the first draft of my book. A nice bargain for both of us.

At the beginning, I had a hard time just using the syllabus to write the book. Too dry—and it even bored me to read what I had written. But, writing about 500 songs through the years and many magazine articles, I was well aware of my "voice," and I decided to apply it to my syllabus. And voilà—suddenly, the book became fun, and I looked forward to working on it. However, what is my "voice"? It's not dry or fussy or overly cerebral and boring; rather, it's "breezy," somewhat like a friend telling you all the exciting things they've just learned. I have read many songwriting books that are overly intellectual and long winded, and I didn't want this one to be one of them. I don't believe being lofty or brainy makes you learn better. And I did not want to be too fanciful, talking about stuff that was too much in the clouds. I like to be down to earth and get into the nuts and bolts.

This book contains the step-by-step "how to" for writing a lyric, but more than that, it talks about what it takes to be a *working songwriter*: how to work with co-writers, how to present your songs, how to network in this industry, and what *not* to do. Being a songwriter is very "people intensive," and through the years, I have observed that the songwriters who are easy to get along with have a better chance of making it.

Writing a lyric is very *personal* and *specific*. And those two words can be very scary to some people. Through the years, I have noticed there are three types of students who come to my classes: one type is totally in touch with their emotions and can easily express them. Then, at the opposite end is the student who, for whatever reasons, is disassociated from their emotions and cannot express them or even "fake them" to write a song. The third type of writer is the most common: this type of writer does a dance with their emotions—sometimes accessing them easily and then, at other times, having to dig deep to find them. The more you write and the more you "dance"—I think it gets easier to tap into the stuff that will communicate what you are feeling. You must have access to and a relationship with your emotions in order to write.

It's valuable to write about the things you may be fearful of saying, but if you do, and you have the techniques to do it well, those scary subjects can have a wonderful chemistry. You will be rewarded for being brave. For, as my late husband used to say, "Life favors the bold."

I can teach almost anyone the techniques of writing, but I've noticed over the years, not everyone has something to say. In the final analysis, that's what makes a writer. And if you *are* a writer, you've got to tell that story or you'll bust—no ifs, ands, or buts: You *have to write that song*, or you'll stop breathing or roll up into a little ball and fade away.

I just wrote a song today and, after all these many years, it was still as exciting, challenging, and amazing as when I started writing. Actually, more so than when I was in my twenties, wearing my mullet and being a waiter in Beverly Hills—now I know what I'm doing. And like every songwriter (trust me on this), this song is the best song I have ever written! I know it is.

Mark Winkler

1
INTRODUCTION

I wish I remembered the name of the guy who saved my songwriting career.

It was a long time ago, about 1974. I've asked a few of my friends, but no one can remember him . . . all I can recall is that he was a crusty, no-nonsense older man. I remember his office was on Sunset Boulevard, but every L.A. music publisher's office was on Sunset in those days.

Up until that time, I had been writing songs without any formal instruction (I'd also learned to play the piano along the way). I already knew the drill and I played and sang him my three songs. To give you an idea of the quality of my material, one song was called "King Kong." Since his secretary or a phone call didn't interrupt my songs, and he didn't cut me off after a verse or two, I thought that maybe this time I'd get somewhere.

After I finished my songs, he looked at me and asked, "Who do you think you write like?" Since I was a middle-class Jewish guy who played the piano and favored the Great American Songbook, I answered, "Randy Newman." I even played this guy "I Want to Be Bored with You," a song that I thought captured Newman's signature jaunty, yet nostalgic chords.

My would-be publisher crossed his arms and said, "No, you're not good enough to be Randy Newman. You need to take some songwriting classes." No coddling from this guy! Naturally, my heart sank, and I went through the seven stages of grief in thirty seconds on a loop—and left the office feeling really mad at this man. Now, I'd like to give him a medal, thank him for being honest with me, and for changing my life.

Mark Winkler at the piano (photo by Angie Slagg, used by permission).

After my ego recovered, I enrolled in this crazy 1970s learning institution called the Sherwood Oaks Experimental College and took my first songwriting class with a seasoned songwriter, Al Kasha, a two-time Academy Award Best Song winner. (You might remember one of those songs, "The Morning After," which was lip-synched by actress Carole Lynley just before the boat sank in *The Poseidon Adventure*.)

Taking Al's class changed my life. It taught me the rules for writing a good song. It also introduced me to three songwriting partners for the next few years (and an ex-girlfriend), but most importantly, it started me on a songwriting journey that I'm still enjoying to this day.

Since I'm probably older than you are and somewhat crusty, perhaps I can do the same for you.

2
A WORKING SONGWRITER

Most of us in the music business start out wanting to become superstars, to sell out stadiums, have legions of social media followers, and to have our every song hit the top of the charts. That's not the way it usually works. Don't get me wrong; I hope you're the next Taylor Swift or Bruno Mars or Ed Sheeran. But there's one thing I can promise you—if you learn your songwriting craft well, have good people skills and work ethics, you will find a place in the music industry. It can be the backup plan your parents are always saying you need. How do I know this? Because it happened to me. When people ask me how I rank in the music business, I always tell them I'm "fame-adjacent."

I grew up in a musical family. My mom, Marceline Marlowe, was a big-band singer and filled my head with dreams of touring with a band, staying up late and eating spareribs with the horn section; you know, the stuff of dreams. My mom's sister, my Aunt Shirley, also was a singer and on most Friday nights, the family would get together around the piano and sing. My mom would usually do "What a Difference a Day Makes" or "Embraceable You"; my Aunt Shirley would belt out "The Man I Love"; my older brother Bob would sing "Because of You" and sometimes my grandmother or grandfather would sing. Grampa Schneider favored Al Jolson songs. Though my mom gave up showbiz to raise a family, she never stopped loving it.

So, no wonder by the time I was nine, I was already dreaming of being a singer and was writing little snippets of songs. Around the time I was in high school, Aunt Shirley discovered I could sing and decided I should meet this guy, Jimmie Haskell, who had played accordion in the Herb Silvers band that she sang with, but who now was a big arranger. He arranged "Bridge Over Troubled Water" for Simon & Garfunkel and "Ode to Billie Joe" for Bobbie Gentry. He also worked with Mama Cass, Jose Feliciano, and The Grass Roots, among others.

Before I knew it, I was at his apartment singing "Goin' Out of My Head" while he accompanied me on a Fender Rhodes electric piano. Jimmie took me under his wing and got me writing songs. They were rather terrible. It was the late 1960s and my songs were somewhat psychedelic retreads of what I was hearing on the radio. Jimmie decided to produce some masters (finished recordings) of two of my songs. I thought it would be no time before my songs were being played on Los Angeles' KHJ "Boss Radio" and I would be touring with Sky Saxon and the Seeds, or Sonny & Cher.

The masters didn't sell, but I started singing with a wedding band in Long Beach and learning a lot of songs. It was in a horn band—because Chicago and Blood, Sweat & Tears were big in those days—and let me tell you, nothing is louder than a horn section when the players are all in their early twenties! I learned that a lot of the lyrics I was singing were fairly bad (I need only to refer you to "Color My World" by Chicago, which makes no literal sense) and I started thinking, "I can do better than this."

That brought me to the publisher's office that drove me to the songwriting class where everything began for me. From there, I started writing with some talented people including Jim Andron, and we started getting some of our songs recorded by LTD and Stephanie Mills. I joined a great songwriting group that met every Monday night at Jim's house, which forged some powerful connections and writing relationships for me.

During this time, I was singing and making demos. I was the bastard pop child of Billy Joel or Barry Manilow. I got some bites, but nothing really happened. One night at the songwriter's group, I played my latest demo, and Jim, my cowriter said, "How nice, you can always count on Mark to be middle-of-the-road." Even though he probably meant it as a compliment, I decided that I was a lot quirkier and more original than that.

Also, during this time, I discovered that the wedding band I was singing with was also a jazz band in the style of Tom Scott and the L.A. Express, and I really dug their tunes. This was at the same time that I discovered a yet-unsigned Al Jarreau at the Bla-Bla Café in the San Fernando Valley, and Manhattan Transfer, and Michael Franks. So, one day while noodling on the piano I came up with an idea for a theme album called *Jazz Life*, where every song would use jazz as a metaphor for life. I was singing a lovely combination of jazz and pop that allowed my lyrics to be deeper and more reflective of who I was. With my songwriting partner Jim Andron, I did a demo of five of our cowritten songs and amazingly, got it signed to a small label in Seattle called First American Records.

When the album came out, it did nicely on jazz stations in the United States. The first time I heard it on our local jazz station KBCA, I was driving on the 405 Freeway in Los Angeles. As a Carmen McRae song ended, I heard the funky little chords of my song "Bebop" and then my voice coming

My first album, Jazz Life *(photo by Orah Moore, used by permission).*

through my car radio. Nothing quite prepares you for hearing your voice on the radio. It sounds eerily familiar, yet somehow different. Of course, I missed my turnoff and got lost for about twenty minutes. It was worth it.

After the release of *Jazz Life*, I didn't become Al Jarreau or the Manhattan Transfer, but the album became a minor classic in Japan, where it was written up in magazines and even in a book as a 1980s jazz classic. So far, it's been rereleased three times in that country. Through the years, I was also signed to two lucrative publishing deals in Japan and have had many of my albums come out on a plethora of labels there. That's the cool thing about show business—it never happens the way you think it will.

During the 1980s and 1990s, while getting some more of my songs recorded and performed by artists like Randy Crawford, Dianne Reeves, and Dee Dee Bridgewater, I began making a name for myself as a singer/songwriter in the mold of Dave Frishberg or Ben Sidran. I started as a lyricist, then became a recording artist/singer-songwriter.

My husband's best friend, Bob Schrock, was the artistic director of a small but plucky gay theater, The Celebration, in L.A. He was having a hard time filling seats, but he noticed every time he did a musical or a show with some nudity, the place was packed! So, one day he came over to dinner and said he had an idea for a new musical revue called *Naked Boys Singing!*

As you'll see later in the book, titles are very important in songs and, as I found out, in naming musicals. If it's as bold and specific as this one is, it can attract and even deliver you an audience. He wanted the show to be a lighthearted musical revue featuring a cast of eight abundantly talented (and naked) guys. I love musicals and was delighted that he wanted me to write some songs for it. Luckily for me, the previous week I had connected with a very talented writer named Shelly Markham who had a lot more experience writing musical numbers than I did. I wound up writing two and a half songs for the show, and Shelly taught me a lot about writing for musicals. I am proud to be part of the group of thirteen extremely talented writers who created the show. The show opened and was a big hit in Los Angeles and in New York.

In the early 2000s, I wrote more musicals. *Play It Cool* also made it to Off Broadway and *Bark* (for which I also wrote the book/script) and *Too Old for the Chorus* have played all over the country. I wrote another show that had a short run in L.A. and one that never got produced.

Poster from Naked Boys Singing *(artwork owned by Michael D'Angora, used by permission).*

CHAPTER 2

Mark (right) with Barbara Morrison (center) and arranger/pianist Eli Brueggemann (left) at the recording of their duet "Sweet Spot" (photo by Richard Del Belso).

As my career as a singer heated up in those days, other jazz singers sought me out to produce their albums and I added "record producer" to my résumé. I also used the independent record label I established, Café Pacific Records, to release some of the singers I produced.

Then, in the middle of writing one of my musicals, I decided to fulfill a lifelong ambition and become a songwriting teacher. To be honest, I didn't know if I had anything to teach, but it didn't take me long to realize that I had thirty years of experience to share. Teaching songwriting has become the most satisfying occupation of all. And to think, I started out just wanting to be a superstar (how boring!).

The bottom line to all of this, the foundation on which it is built, is knowing how to write a good commercial song. It's helped me in each new profession I've undertaken. If you know the elements of a good song, and you can

Mark (back row, fourth on the left) with UCLA class (photo by Mark Winkler with students' permissions).

spot one when you hear it, you can go a long way. Just think of Clive Davis. The recording and entertainment industry is built on great songs.

I say I'm "fame-adjacent" because "the people who know" probably know my name and respect me. I usually get good reviews, in the musical theater world everyone knows *Naked Boys Singing!*, and in my world of jazz and jazz singers, I'm a legit star.

I've been teaching lyric writing for over twenty years, over eighteen years at the UCLA Extension, and over ten years at the Songwriting School of Los Angeles; this is after shorter stints at the Learning Annex and the Songwriters Guild. This book is based on the syllabi I created to teach lyric writing for these institutions. Over the years I've refined it and fleshed it out to teach my students in a way that I hope is down-to-earth and fun. I've never been one to lecture in "professor-speak." As in songwriting, I like to use a conversational language that is easily understood, and I will attempt to do the same in this book.

While I've never had anyone like Bruno or Taylor in my classes, I am proud that my students have gone on to enjoy solid careers in show business. They write for animated movies, cowrite hit songs, have become powerful agents and publishers, sing in Academy Award–winning movies, and put out a lot of great indie albums!

So, now that you know a little bit more about me—let's write a lyric!

3
HOW TO JUDGE IF YOUR LYRIC IS GOOD

A few years ago, I had a young woman in my class who was a triple threat: a singer, dancer, and writer—very much in the mold of Beyoncé.

It seemed that every week she was riding a different emotion as she prepared for class. One week, her songs were as good as Beyoncé's and Sia's. The next, her songwriting was terrible, and she felt worthless.

Emotions are a wonderful thing to tap into when writing your songs, but a bad thing when you are evaluating your work. In my opinion, she was a talented woman who was learning the craft of songwriting. Her efforts were inconsistent, which is the norm in the first stages of learning how to write songs. I remember sitting her down and telling her the good news: there is a way to tell if your song works or not. Writing a song is not like inventing the wheel; it's a process that's been done almost the same way since the first decade of the twentieth century.

What changes in songs is the vernacular (the way we speak, the slang and phrases we use currently), instrumentation, rhythm, and subject matter. Of course, most songs are about love. But the song lyric is considerably tied in with the times it is written, and the times keep on "a-changing"—as Dylan so beautifully put it. For example, from the 1920s until the 1960s, it was perfectly acceptable for a woman to sing about loving a man who cheated on her and even beat her (e.g., "My Man," "Bill," or "Black Coffee"). Today, that stance is unacceptable, and almost ludicrous, to a modern audience.

Winkler digresses . . .

When I was a young songwriter, I remember going to see hit tunesmith Barry Mann being interviewed. He, with his wife and lyricist, Cynthia Weil, have written such classics as "On Broadway," "Just Once," and "You've Lost That Lovin' Feelin'." The interviewer asked him how he went about writing a song, and he replied he didn't know, and that he never even knew if he was going to write another song again. I started shaking in my young songwriter boots! Here's this veteran songwriter—and he doesn't even know if he's going to write another song. However, now that I've been writing for quite a long time, I think Barry was artistically fibbing just a little, or maybe for his particular psychology to work, it was glamorous and a little bit dangerous to not know when his next song would appear. And honestly, sometimes artists don't like to reveal how the magic is made.

Mark (center) with Barry Mann (right) and Cynthia Weil (left) at the L.A. opening of Play It Cool (photo by Richard Del Belso).

HOW TO JUDGE IF YOUR LYRIC IS GOOD

This book will teach you the ways to write a good lyric and provide you with the criteria to judge whether your song is good or not. When I was a new songwriter, it would bother me when my songs were inconsistent and just "laid there." I knew my lyric wasn't working, but I didn't know how to fix it.

I had just written a lyric for a wonderful melody by David Benoit titled "Land of the Loving," which was sung by Dianne Reeves on David's breakout album *This Side Up*, and I was riding high. Then, David asked me to write another lyric for his next album and I wrote a turkey, which he didn't record. I remember looking at it and not knowing how to fine-tune it. Now, I realize the song was lacking some of the techniques needed to make it really good.

So, through writing and teaching songwriting these many years, I've added quite a few tools to my tool belt I'd like to share with you.

Here are some of the things you will learn:

What a verse must accomplish
What a chorus must accomplish
Different kinds of rhyme
Prosody
Specificity
Repetition
Writing lyrics to a melody
Where the title should appear in the song
Having a consistent tone
Telling a compelling story
Using alliteration and anaphora
Being conversational
How to be authentic and believable
Knowing who is singing and who they are singing to
Knowing what your song must accomplish
Lyrical hooks in addition to the title
Picture words

Knowing these techniques of songwriting gives you the criteria to go beyond your emotions and see if your song has the stuff it takes to work in the viable marketplace—to be "good."

4

COME UP WITH A GREAT TITLE

The first step I take when I'm beginning to write a song is to come up with the title.

One of the fastest ways I know I'm working with an amateur songwriter is when I ask for the song title and they say, "I don't know" or, "I haven't come up with it yet." Know this: successful songwriters, from Sza to Post Malone, start with the title.

Why is that so?

A great title is more than half the battle in songwriting because

- It tells you what to write;
- It attracts your listener because it's catchy;
- It's specific; it sets the direction of the song;
- It can contain alliteration, pictures, unique elements, and/or a surprise to get the listener hooked;
- And much like the name for a cologne, a car, or a cereal, clever song titles can "brand" a singer.

From this minute on, start a title folder on your phone, on your computer, or even in an old-school notebook. Whenever something strikes you as interesting, write it down.

Here are examples of some of my favorite song titles:

- Justin Timberlake's "SexyBack"

This was his first big song as a grown man and not just a member of a boy band. The song, written with Timbaland, was a little experimental, a little dangerous, basically announcing that Mr. Timberlake was back and sexy. It became his first number one single on the Billboard Hot 100 and is one of the best-selling singles of the first decade of the 2000s.

Each of these song titles branded the singers as future superstars, illustrated their personas, and introduced them to the public:

- Billie Eilish's "Bad Guy"
- Barbra Streisand's "I'm the Greatest Star"
- Lizzo's "Truth Hurts"
- Madonna's "Material Girl"
- Jennifer Lopez's "Jenny from the Block"
- Pink's "Don't Let Me Get Me"

Here are some examples of titles that are surprising and spark curiosity:

- "Die a Happy Man" won the 2016 CMA Single of the Year for Thomas Rhett.
- "That's What I Like," a huge hit for Bruno Mars, and was the Song of the Year at the 2018 GRAMMY Awards.
- "Shape of You" was a huge international hit for Ed Sheeran.
- "Watermelon Sugar" is a very provocative title by Harry Styles.
- "My Life Would Suck without You" was a 2009 megahit for Kelly Clarkson.
- "All About That Bass" made a name for 2014 newcomer Meghan Trainor.
- "The Bones" by Maren Morris was a hit on both pop and country charts in 2020.
- "hot girl bummer" is a song you can't get out of your mind and in the summer of 2020 this was it by Blackbear.
- "Unbreak My Heart," Diane Warren's power ballad, became a huge hit for Toni Braxton—notice the title isn't, "Please Mend My Heart," which would have made just as much sense, but is not half as catchy.

COME UP WITH A GREAT TITLE   17

- "Who Let the Dogs Out," was a one-hit wonder for the Baha Men in 2000. Through the years, every time I say the title in class, it gets a laugh. "Funny" is a great quality in a title.

Single-word titles have always been popular. Single words are punchy, concise, and in our short-attention-span society, seem perfect:

- BTS' "Dynamite"
- Imagine Dragons' "Believer"
- Lorde's "Royals"
- Post Malone's "Circles"
- Miranda Lambert's "Bluebird"
- Megan Thee Stallion's (featuring Beyoncé) "Savage"
- Kendrick Lamar's "HUMBLE"
- Pharrell Williams' "Happy"

Country songs have some of the best titles:

- Sam Hunt's "Body Like a Back Road"
- Ashley McBryde's "One Night Standards"
- Jordan Davis's "Slow Dancing in a Parking Lot"
- Toby Keith's "Beer for My Horses"
- Joe Nichols's "She Only Smokes When She Drinks"
- Miranda Lambert's "Crazy Ex-Girlfriend"
- Kenny Chesney's "She Thinks My Tractor's Sexy"

And then there are "bad titles." These are titles that don't do you any favors as a songwriter. They tend to be generic.* They don't seem to suggest a story. They don't make the listener curious. I'm not saying you can't write a good song from them; I'm just saying you have to work twice as hard to do so. Here are some examples:

- "I Love You"
- "I Need You"
- "You Look Nice"
- "Happy Times"

- "Just Because"
- "Thinking of Things"
- "Days"

Since they're generic, there will be hundreds of songs of the same title, opening you to the possibility of mistakes in reporting from your performing rights royalties (despite metadata).

INSPIRATION FOR TITLES

Here are some overall thoughts about where to look for ideas. Generally, you can't copyright a title. The only book title I've heard about that is copyrighted is *Valley of the Dolls* and that's because Jacqueline Susann coined the phrase "dolls" to mean "pills," that is, the uppers and downers Neely O'Hara took so many of in the book.

But know that the titles of books, movies, and songs are pretty much yours for the taking. As you can see from the following examples, everything old is new again.

Song Titles

The title "Crazy" has been used in altogether different hit songs for Patsy Cline, Kenny Rogers, Aerosmith, Seal, and CeeLo Green.

"Dancing in the Dark" was a hit in the forties by Dietz and Schwartz and in the eighties written by Bruce Springsteen.

"Time after Time" was a hit in the forties by Sammy Cahn and Jule Styne and a different one in the eighties composed by Cyndi Lauper and Rob Hyman.

[Note to the readers: These are different songs and because of the same title, problems could arise when paying royalties—see note above.]

Books

I love to go into my favorite bookstore to check out the book titles. I always find at least five I can put in my title folder. Many years ago, I saw an autobiography of former television star Brett Butler titled *Knee Deep in Paradise* and I quickly wrote down the title. I never did write a lyric to it, so it's yours. I also always check out the Sunday edition of *The New York Times* bestseller lists for titles.

Movies

I also use Netflix, Amazon, and other streaming services to look for old movie titles. They are there for the taking. I love film noir and a few years ago fell in love with this great 1953 Humphrey Bogart movie called *In a Lonely Place*. When I finished watching the movie, I started writing a theme song for it, using the themes of the movie to craft one of my favorite songs that I have ever written. I wrote it with the wonderful Marilyn Harris and it can be found on two of my albums: *Till I Get It Right* and *West Coast Cool*. I've been lucky to have about half a dozen people record it over the years.

It's fun to write a theme song for a movie. And it's a good exercise, because the movie will give you everything you need to write a song—its title and its themes.

Television and Movie Dialogue

I've heard that Babyface watches soap operas and gets many of his song ideas from them. I once got a title from a line Kevin Bacon's character said in *Footloose*. He was talking about a girl with his friend and he asked, "She ever get busted for boppin'?," implying he liked his girls a little dangerous. (You can find my song "Busted for Boppin'" on my album *Ebony Rain* and on Full Swing's *In Full Swing* album on Cypress Records.)

Eavesdropping

I admit it, I love to order an espresso at my local coffee house and sit next to interesting people and listen to what they have to say. Some people actually talk in song titles—I could write a whole paragraph on this—but needless to say, it doesn't take long to figure out if the conversation is "title-worthy" or not. If it isn't, move, and find a more interesting conversation.

Ripped from the Headlines

At the top of newspaper or magazine articles—including articles on the internet—there are always attention-getting, catchy, and memorable head- lines—just like the title of your songs should be. I love looking through *People* magazine and HuffPost.com. Here are some examples: "Torn Between Two Lovers," "I Woke Up Married to a Stranger," "Where Are They Now?," and "The Sky Is Not My Limit."

Writing the Story of the Title

Once you've come up with a title you like, then come up with a story to fit the title. You must be able to tell the story of your song in two or three sentences.

Take Charlie Rich's 1973 hit "Behind Closed Doors." The story was a guy telling the world that he had a lover who was a lady in public, but who loved him like nobody's business when they got up close and personal. Songs are basically simple creatures that tell us one story very well.

Meghan Trainor's aforementioned "All About That Bass" is about a full-figured woman telling other women that while she has a big "bass," she owns the way she looks, and, by the way, the men like it too. She throws in a great metaphor—that's comparing something to another thing that isn't connected—like comparing her booty to a bass.

In "Take Me to Church," Hozier does one of the most surefire things there is to do in pop music: he mixes sex and religion. Just ask Prince, Madonna, Dusty Springfield, Little Richard, or Bon Jovi; it's worked for them too. The story of the song is basically Hozier telling everybody that he wants to worship at the altar of his girlfriend, who's better at taking him to heaven than any Sunday morning preacher.

I wrote a song called "Scattin' in the Moonlight" that's about a guy telling his friend that the thing that makes him love his girlfriend the most is the thing she doesn't even know he sees and hears. Pretty provocative. But, in the case of this song, it's the way she secretly scats like Ella Fitzgerald when she's listening to jazz.

All of these song's title plots can be told in two sentences.

SONGWRITING ACTIONS

Come up with ten titles. Four of them have to be "picture titles," which is a title you can see. For example, "Little Red Corvette," "Raining in My Heart," and "Beer for My Horses."

- Make them interesting.
- Make us curious.
- Make them provocative.
- Make them catchy.

And if you can point us to the story of the song, that would be great.

However...

Always look for a title that gives you an emotional ping. No matter how great your title is, if you don't feel it, your audience won't either. As a songwriter, you need to write what you know and can feel deeply in your heart. It doesn't have to be serious though. (One of my favorite songs written in my class was about "Iced Frappuccinos.") The songwriter really dug drinking them and was able to transfer her enthusiasm and delight into her lyrics in a big way.

Once you have ten titles, take two that you like the best and write a two-sentence description of the story the song tells.

5

SONG FORMS

Congratulations! Now you've got some titles and a two-sentence description of the stories your songs will tell.

When I first started teaching, one of the things I discovered quickly is that people who thoroughly understand song form, and what each section of the song must accomplish, become better lyricists and songwriters faster. Don't expect yourself to know all this material in one sitting; songwriting is a process. It's only by writing songs, making mistakes, and realizing when you aren't following the rules, that you'll become better. Yes, there are exceptions to the rules. But songwriting is a very concise form—there's not a lot of space to get your story across—so more than 95 percent of popular songs follow the rules fairly closely.

Another interesting phenomenon I've noticed as a teacher is that just by looking at the lyric sheets that my students hand in, I can tell rapidly if they understand song form. If the sections of the song don't match or don't contrast where they should, I can see quickly there is a problem.

Unconsciously, most listeners have been trained to expect where the different elements of the song must take them. After all, writers have been writing with the two most popular forms since the beginning of the twentieth century. So, if you as the writer don't deliver that to them, they will become confused or bored and move on to the next song. Having the correct form plays a major role in writing a good song.

Your next step is to take one of your titles and the story description, then decide what form you'll use for your song. For most pop, hip-hop, electronic dance music, urban, and country songs, "verse/chorus" is the most popular form. However, for musical theater, cabaret, jazz, and some country compositions, the predominating form is AABA. It's the form most often used for the Great American Songbook.

A LITTLE MUSICAL HISTORY

In 1954, American music changed radically. "Race music" had morphed into R&B and became a strong influence in rock and roll, country songs started to cross over into pop. Soon enough, baby boomer teens soured on the novelty songs of the early 1950s (think "How Much Is That Doggie in the Window?") and overly crafted Great American Songbook-inspired hits (like "Love Is a Many-Splendored Thing") and latched onto the exciting and urgent sentiments of Elvis, Little Richard, Chuck Berry, and Jerry Lee Lewis.

These songs were brash, sexual, and the form was verse/chorus. Songwriters learned they could repeat their hooks, put in more hooks, and do it faster, if the song had a chorus. And the "almost rhymes" and "raw words" of this new style of song weren't so highfalutin as the high-toned work of aging writers of the Great American Songbook.

It's a fascinating subject. For many years, rock and roll was portrayed as the devil and many sidelined writers of the Great American Songbook became bitter and felt irrelevant. In the end, the verse/chorus form won the rivalry and became the formula for popular song.

VERSE/CHORUS
- Verse #1
- Verse #2
- Chorus #1
- Verse #3
- Chorus #2
- Bridge
- Chorus #3

SONG FORMS

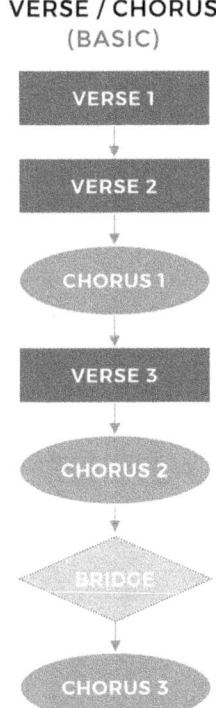

Here's what each section must accomplish:

Verse #1
Before you even start writing, ask yourself three important questions that will focus your lyrics:

- Who is singing?
- Who are they singing to?
- What is the singer/narrator trying to accomplish?

With those questions answered, you can set up the story, the rhyme scheme (which lines you are rhyming), and set the tone of the song. It's important to know that each verse of the song has the same melody, give or take an eighth or sixteenth note. The *scansion* of the song (the rhythm and length of the line) must match in each verse. You can also imply or state time of day and location in the first verse lyrics. Oh, and not all lines of a song are created equal. The first line of your first verse is one of the most important lines in a song, so make it a good one.

Chorus #1

This is where the hook is! Lyrically, the chorus essentially summarizes what the song is about. It doesn't further the story at all.

Recently, the chorus has been divided into two sections: the first part is the title hook and summarization of the theme and the second part, often called the post-chorus, contains a nonsense syllable (called a *vocable*) or a vocal chop (a heavily processed vocal or musical line) or some other hook that can be placed in the song. The chorus should have a different rhyme scheme than the verse. The scansion of the chorus should be markedly different than the verse. If the lines of your verse are long, try varying the rhythm and making the chorus lines shorter. Usually, the melody line is higher in pitch in the chorus than in the verses

Verse #2

Verse #2 "continues" the story; it does not repeat the old information. Melodically it matches the first verse and, in a perfect world, it repeats the rhyme scheme.

Chorus #2

Just repeat the first chorus—easy. In most forms of popular music, the melody and lyrics remain the same in the chorus, with only minor variations. In musical theater, the lyrics in the chorus can change to further the story.

Bridge

This is the change-up; you can change the rhythm of the lines, the narrator (if you're in first person in the verse/chorus—you can be second person in the bridge, or you can change tenses). Going from present to past, "I remember when we . . . ," or future, "Someday we will . . ." The bridge builds to the last chorus—it's a change in pace and perspective. You can also put the philosophy of the tune in the bridge. It's my favorite part of the song because you can be very creative with the scansion, rhythm, and point of view.

SONG FORMS

Chorus #3
Just repeat the first and second chorus.

VERSE/CHORUS, THE DELUXE VERSION
- Verse #1
- Pre-chorus #1
- Chorus #1
- Verse #2
- Pre-chorus #2
- Chorus #2
- Bridge
- Pre-chorus #3
- Chorus #3

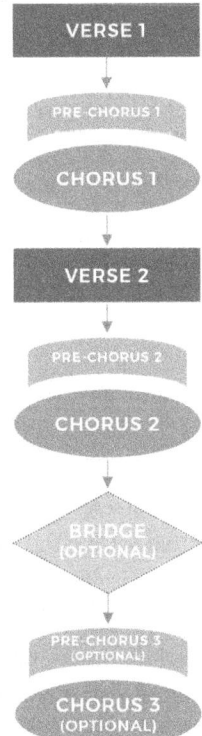

Pre-chorus

The requirements for this are the same as your "basic" verse/chorus, but now you have a new section just before the chorus. Why is it so popular? You guessed it; you can put more "hooks" into it. For example, Lorde, in her song, "Royals," has a very catchy laundry list pre-chorus, before her first chorus.

The pre-chorus furthers the story. It builds to the chorus and is a variation from the verse (both in rhythm pattern, scansion, and rhyming). Most importantly, it can contain a new hook—or phrase that's catchy. Because the pre-chorus gives you more melodic variation, you may not need a bridge in this song form.

AABA

AABA is the primary form of the Great American Songbook classics, which lasted generally from the twenties until the mid-fifties with the advent of rock and roll. The last AABA songs in pop music are "What Was I Made For?" from the movie *Barbie* by Billie Eilish, "Hey Delilah" by the Plain White T's, "Every Breath You Take" by The Police, and "Don't Know Why" by Norah Jones.

AABA
- Verse (optional)
- A #1
- A #2
- B #1
- A #3
- B #2
- A #4

Verse (optional)

This is nothing like the verse in a verse/chorus song. It comes before the first A. It is an introductory section that sets up the song. It comes from the recitative in opera or operetta, which basically is musicalized dialogue leading to the aria. Most of the Great American Songbook songs had them (although not all singers choose to sing them). But in the very economical and concise AABA form, sometimes you can use all the lines you can get. For example, listen to the film version of "Over the Rainbow" sung by Judy Garland in *The*

Wizard of Oz. You will hear that this version begins with the lyric, "When all the world is a hopeless jumble . . ." That is the verse, now rarely sung, but lovely to hear.

A #1

This is where you place the title (hook or refrain). You place it in the first or last line of each A section. Just like the verse in a verse/chorus song, this is where you ask the following questions:

- Who is singing?
- Who are they singing to?
- What are they trying to accomplish?

Then you set up the story, the rhyme scheme (which lines you're rhyming, doing inner rhymes, etc.), and set the tone of the tune. It's important to know that each "A" section of the song has the same melody, give or take an eighth or sixteenth note. The "scansion" of the song (the rhythm and length of the line) must match in each "A" section. You can also imply or state time of day and location in the first "A" lyrics. So, all of the things you need to do in a verse you need to do in the first "A," but you just don't have as much space, after all, you've got to get the title of the song in there.

As a rule, AABA is less wordy than verse/chorus—with not that many lines to get across what you want to say. However, there have been some magnificent songs written in this form such as Kern and Harbach's "Smoke Gets in Your Eyes," the abovementioned "Over the Rainbow" by Arlen and Harburg, and Rodgers and Hart's "Where or When," to only mention three out of thousands.

A #2

This continues the story. You place the title in the first line or last line of the A. You continue the rhyme scheme and the scansion of the song. You do not repeat any information you have already written in the first "A" section.

Bridge

Much the same as a bridge in a verse/chorus song, it's a change-up. You change the scansion of the tune, the rhyme scheme. You can change your "person" or "tense" and it must build toward the last "A" section. It can contain the philosophy of the song and it can also look at things from a slightly different angle.

A #3

It's just like "A" #2. Once again, you are continuing the story. But sometimes in AABA songs such as, "The Way We Were," by Marvin Hamlisch and Marilyn and Alan Bergman, the last "A" changes melody and form slightly to dramatically come to a finish. Sometimes, as in John Phillips's "California Dreamin'," and John Denver's "Annie's Song," the "A" #3 is just the first "A" repeated. It's a nice bookend and a form of repetition.

"That's why I say": A fun trick to see if your chorus is working

After you finish your verse or pre-chorus and are ready to go into the chorus, say "That's why I say" before you sing your chorus lyrics. And then if the lyrics make sense following "That's why I say," your chorus does what it needs to do and is correct.

The "That's why I say" isn't part of your lyric; it's just something you utter under your breath while writing the song. And it works!

For example, in one of the greatest songs of the twentieth century, "You've Lost That Lovin' Feelin" by Barry Mann and Cynthia Weil, use my trick: say "That's why I say" between the pre-chorus and the beginning of the chorus and it makes perfect sense.

Here's a link to the lyric: https://www.streetdirectory.com/lyricadvisor/song/wlffjj/youve_lost_that_lovin_feelin/.

SONGWRITING ACTIONS

Now that you know the song forms, pick your best title. How do you do that (see chapter 4)? Choose the catchiest title that makes you most curious to hear the song. The title and story/plot must deliver an emotional ping to you.

Then come up with a story based on your title. You should be able to tell your story in two to three lines.

SONG FORMS

Pick your song form:
If you're pop, urban hip-hop, singer/songwriter, or rock: *pick verse/chorus*
If you're musical theater, jazz, or cabaret: *pick AABA*
If you're country: *you can choose either one*

Then, write a lyric for the song utilizing your title, story, and chosen song form.

OBJECTIVES OF THE SONGWRITING ACTIONS
To turn your title and story into a song utilizing the form you have picked.

6
BE SPECIFIC

To me, *specificity* is the most important ingredient in writing song lyrics. It lends your song "authenticity" and emotional weight.

Take "authenticity" first: authenticity means being real, verifiable, and honest. One of the most important qualities reflected in a lyric is that we believe the singer who's singing the song. You don't want to throw your support behind an artist who's not "real." Think of some of the more recent great writers: Amy Winehouse, Taylor Swift, and Ed Sheeran. You might like them or not, but we never question that they mean what they write and sing.

What specifically are specifics?

Imagine yourself living with a roommate in Hollywood, and you go out on a date with a great guy. Your roommate's waiting up when you get home—she's perched on the side of the bed, and she wants to hear all the details. You say, "Hey I'm really tired, I'll tell you all about it in the morning." But your roommate won't take "no" for an answer. She looks at the clock and says, "It's 11:28, it's not even midnight yet." So, you tell her that he took you to dinner at the Musso & Frank Grill, really old-school with white tablecloths and waiters who looked like they were about eighty. Then you mention that after the Welsh rarebit, lettuce wedge, and Latin Manhattan, you went up to the lobby of the Hollywood Roosevelt Hotel to hear your friend Mark Winkler sing (okay, I'm shameless, as if you hadn't guessed). Mark was so good you stayed for a few songs in the second set. Your roommate seems satisfied with the "details" and you go to sleep.

The morning comes and so do two hard-boiled detectives from Hollywood homicide division. They ask you if you went out with the abovementioned great guy, and you say "yes." They tell you he's been murdered, and they want to know what time you came home. Your roommate chimes in 11:28 p.m. and then explains why she knows the exact time. The police thank you and leave.

You see, the great guy was murdered after 2:00 a.m., so you're not a suspect. All the details your roommate supplied made them believe her—and you. The same thing applies to lyrics. If you're vague and nondescriptive, nobody will believe you and you'll be guilty as charged. Come up with compelling details and you're home free.

Specificity also gives your lyrics emotional weight. This is where one of my students usually asks, "But if the lyric is too 'specific,' won't I lose a lot of my audience?" The answer is "no," because specificity is just a portal into a greater emotional truth that we all can share.

All the accoutrements just make the story more vivid and interesting. We all know that Taylor Swift is talking about her life and career when she sings about shaking off the haters because "the haters gonna hate, hate, hate." Most of us don't have the level of fame Taylor has, with legions of followers, bodyguards, and trollers—but we've all been judged harshly from time to time, and maybe even put on the spot: that's the universal emotion we can share.

I love the lyrics of the Alan Jackson song "Drive (For Daddy Gene)," about a son learning from his father how to drive a motorboat and then a hand-me-down Ford with a dent on the side. As the song goes on, the son grows up and teaches his daughters how to drive a Jeep.

The first time I heard the last line of the tune, "It's just an old plywood boat with a 75 Johnson electric choke," I had to pull over to the side of the road, I was crying so much. Hell, I'm not a country boy, I've hardly ever been in a boat, and I definitely wouldn't know what kind of motor a "75 Johnson" is, even if I fell over it. But the intense specificity of the song reminded me of my dad and the things he taught me as a young man, and then how I've passed his lessons on to so many people in my life. If Alan Jackson didn't write with such detail, I wouldn't have believed him nor been so captured by the song.

To find the lyrics for "Drive," copy this link:
https://tinyurl.com/yeusk9sz

"Moon River," with music by Henry Mancini and lyrics by Johnny Mercer, shows how a single, specific word can turn a sweet song into an Academy Award–winning standard. The song was featured in the charming 1961 movie *Breakfast at Tiffany's*, in which Audrey Hepburn played Holly Golightly, a country girl who's run away from a small Southern town to the big, bad city of New York, where she's dressed by Givenchy and jeweled by Tiffany's—basically, a very high-class call girl. She's fine with her lot, until she falls in love with a handsome yet very nice guy (played by George Peppard) and starts to question her life choices.

So, she does what any country girl would do: puts on a gingham shirt, ties her hair up in pigtails, and goes out to the fire escape to play her guitar and serenade us with a little tune about where she's been and where she hopes to go.

"Moon River"
We're after the same rainbow's end . . .
My _____ friend, Moon River and me

In the lyric, she doesn't sing, "my good-old country friend" or "gee, you're such a friend," although both are correct descriptions with the right number of syllables for the melody. But they are vague or even worse, generic. She sings:

My huckleberry friend,

Much better choice! Huckleberries grow by the river, and a country girl would know that. It also brings up thoughts of Huckleberry Finn, who took to the river to escape his small-town lot in life, so it sounds authentic, unique, and specific—it even rolls off the tongue nicely. Just one perfect adjective adds so much to this song. Sometimes great songwriting all boils down to one word that lifts a song to a whole new level.

As I like to say in my classes, it's not just any place, it's "Under the Boardwalk," "Down in the Boondocks," "Summer in the City," "In the Ghetto," or at a "Stoned Soul Picnic."

Amy Winehouse didn't get sober, she went to "Rehab."

And it's not just any time, it's the "Time of Your Life," it's "'Round Midnight," it's "Manic Monday," and it's "Suppertime."

Also, it's not just any night! It's "Southern Nights," "Tropical Nights," "The Hottest Night of the Year," "December, 1963 (Oh, What a Night)," and "The Night the Lights Went Out in Georgia."

Use strong, descriptive adjectives, clever combinations of nouns and verbs—in Nashville, they call this "furniture." Here's a song of mine with a lot of furniture. I wrote it with Marilyn Harris, and it can be found on my album *The Company I Keep*.

"That Afternoon in Harlem"
Lyrics by Mark Winkler

Verse #1
Her apartment was smaller than I remembered,
Though it had a grand piano tucked inside.
　Winkler: Nice specific on the piano, I like the word "tucked" as the verb
The place was stuffed with old knick-knacks,
　Descriptive verb "stuffed" followed by the specific things in the apartment
A gold LP and photographs,
And the occasional poster with her name.

Verse #2
She was the songbird of her generation;
　Tells us who she was, sounds old-fashioned
A jazz singer who toured most of her life.
But now she sat in a well-stuffed chair,
　Good specific adjective
Like an exiled queen with silver hair,
　Nice image with a lot of detail
And regaled me with the stories of her fame.
Once again, "regaled" sounds old and like a visiting dignitary

Chorus #1
And on that afternoon in Harlem,
　Gives you time and location
She sang me a song that she'd made famous.

And though her voice was shot,
> *Strong word, a little harsh*
For a moment, the world just fell away.
> *Nice visual, cinematic and dramatic*

SONGWRITING ACTIONS

Here are three popular songs for you to analyze for "specificity" or "furniture," which are detailed: adjectives, nouns, and verbs in a sentence. Underline the words that are most specific in the song.

"Castle on the Hill" by Ed Sheeran
To find the lyric, please copy this link:
lyricsfreak.com/e/ed+sheeran/castle+on+the+hill_21112527.html

- Notice that he tells you how old he was when he broke his leg
- How fast he was driving down country lanes
- The song he was singing while he was driving

"Fancy" by Bobbie Gentry (as sung by Reba McIntyre)
To find the lyric, please copy this link:
https://genius.com/Reba-mcentire-fancy-lyrics

- Notice that she tells you how old she is and where she lives at the beginning of the song; the state and type of dwelling
- She describes the dress her mama puts on her
- She tells us what crawls across the toe of her shoe (probably one of my favorite pieces of furniture of all time!)

"Fancy Like" by Walker Hayes
To find the lyric, please copy this link:
https://genius.com/Walker-hayes-fancy-like-lyrics

- Notice he tells you what restaurant he takes his girlfriend to when he has a little extra money
- He tells you what he orders in detail
- And he tells us specifically what they do on the way home

7

TOP TEN TIPS FOR LYRIC WRITERS: TIPS 1-5

1. Come up with a great title (see chapter 3)

2. It's the music, stupid
As much as we lyricists love to think we're magicians, if the music is bad, the lyric can't save it. That's just reality. The only exception I can think of is country story songs—if the lyric is stellar, the melody can just be serviceable.

Therefore, what do you do? You'd better be a wonderful lyric writer. Melody writers are more in demand than we lyricists in the music business. Why? They are usually multi-hyphenates who can do arrangements, excel as instrumentalists, and own a well-appointed home studio. The lyricist just has . . . words. So, to get a melody writer's attention, your words need to be terrific. You've got to know your craft backward and forward.

When I started writing with Atlanta native Dean Gant, a terrific musician and writer who had hits with such artists as Anita Baker and Peabo Bryson, he was blown away that my lyrics first had form, made sense, and didn't need a lot of rewriting. It made his life easier. And he liked it that when he gave me a melody first, I could write to that as well. Versatility is a great asset in show biz. And the melody he gave me, "Can't Stand the Pain," became a mid-charting R&B hit for Randy Crawford. I wrote it in three hours walking from Greenwich Village to Midtown Manhattan one magical day while vacationing in New York. This was the eighties and he couldn't believe it when I faxed him the lyric (oh, the good old days!).

As Al Kasha, my first lyric writing teacher and winner of two Academy Awards, said: "A great melody can take you into the top ten, but a great lyric coupled with a great melody will allow you to stay there."

Especially in pop, the melody and title rule. There are many examples in pop music songs that have great melodies, hooks, and ear candy that don't particularly have good lyrics. But the melody combined with killer hooks and great vocals can make a song a winner.

3. Be specific (see chapter 5)

4. A song is not a poem

Do you write poetry? I don't mean to be a spoilsport here, but that doesn't mean you can write a song. Poems and songs are two very unique creatures. One of the easiest ways I know to spot if a lyricist is an amateur is if the person tells me they put their poetry to music. Poetry and lyrics have many things in common, such as cadence (the rhythm of the line), rhyme, metaphor (raining cats and dogs, heart of gold), simile (stars like diamonds), and alliteration. However, there are many differences.

A lyric is designed to be sung, not read. Your lyrics must fit the melody of the song. More about that in the tip below: "Your lyrics must sing and be conversational."

Poetry has many forms; songs use two forms primarily: Verse/Chorus and AABA.

A song needs to be understood quickly; essentially, the first time you hear it. A song can't have fuzzy metaphors, multiple syllables, or hard-to-pronounce consonants that the singer may trip over. No matter how beautifully your words may read, if they can't be sung, they're not lyrics.

5. Your lyrics must sing and be conversational

This would seem to be a no-brainer, but the more I do this thing called songwriting, the more I realize prosody is as important as "content"—and sometimes in pop, it matters more.

Prosody is the way the lyricist sets the words to the melody. Do the words sound good being sung? Sometimes in pop music, that's all you need! I call nonsense lyrics—words or sentences that sound good, but mean virtually nothing—"phrase throwing." I could give you a million examples:

"Watermelon Sugar" comes to mind, as does "Islands in the Stream," or any song written by the Stone Temple Pilots.

Your lyric must be "conversational"—using the language of conventional speech, while matching the stresses and unique qualities of the melody.

You don't want to use a lot of big words for their sake or use words not commonly used or bend your syntax to fit your rhymes. All these things make the listeners have to think about what the singer is singing.

While writing a song, I always speak or sing the words to an imaginary person—picturing an actual friend who is just past my "drishti" (that's a word used in yoga for "gaze"). And if I put "drishti" in a song without putting it in context, I would be stopping my lyric from being conversational.

If you hit a high note in a song, always put it on an open vowel.

Generally, you put your important words on quarter and half notes and leave conjunctions (words such as, and, if, but) to eighth and sixteenth notes. Carefully match the direction of your music and the lyric context: for instance, if the melody is rising, don't have your lyric saying "I'm falling down" with the word "down" being on the highest note.

Winkler digresses . . .

One of my favorite recent musicals is Wicked, *with words and music by Stephen Schwartz who is a master of his craft, but at the end of the second act he* almost *blew it. Okay, he blew it. The green-skinned Elphaba (with more high Cs than anybody should possess) was singing this great song "Defying Gravity," while rising high above the theater. She's singing about finally embracing her dark side when she belts out that nobody is ever going to bring me "down!" on the highest note of the line.*

I told you Stephen was a master, so after she belts that line, she then does a wordless melodic line that's (guess what?) even higher! That's why I say, he almost saved it. The rhyme was "renown" with "down." He could have come up with something, I'm sure. But he settled for a melismatic phrase (singing a word or a single wordless phrase on a succession of notes) to save himself.

While we're on Broadway: Andrew Lloyd Webber—no slouch—and his lyricist Don Black wrote a musical called *Sunset Boulevard*. Maybe because they were Brits, they put the accent on the wrong syllable in the title song. The cast was singing "Sun-SET Boulevard" over and over and the L.A. audience was laughing openly. Why? Because people don't talk that way in Los Angeles, home of the storied SUN-set Boulevard and the setting of the musical. It let us know there was something inauthentic about the song.

And the moral is . . . put the stress on the right syllables, because once again your lyric should be the singer just "talking" to you, telling their story.

8

REWRITING THE BEATLES, AND OTHER THINGS

That visual artists learn their craft by using a great master's work as a tool is nothing new. When I was in Amsterdam at the Rijksmuseum, I was fascinated to see that the great painter Rembrandt did many copies of works by artists he admired, such as Caravaggio and Titian, to learn their techniques. Paul Gauguin reproduced paintings by Van Gogh, and Andy Warhol studied his young contemporary Basquiat to see what he could learn, which resulted in their collaborative canvases.

Using great songs as a template for your own songs is a valuable tool for any songwriter. There's always a reason a song is a hit, and a great song has "great bones." So, why don't you go to the top, and *rewrite* The Beatles, who are undoubtedly (at least in my mind) the most significant pop group of the twentieth century. John Lennon, Paul McCartney, and George Harrison wrote dozens of excellent songs during their quite short tenure as The Beatles. The song of choice to use as a template in this chapter—"Penny Lane."

The lyrics of "Penny Lane" are basically childhood reminiscences, told through a series of vignettes. Each verse contains a vignette, and the last verse brings some of the characters from the earlier verses together in a final scene.

My office and piano, and for inspiration, pictures of The Beatles (photo by Mark Winkler).

Winkler digresses . . .

In the early seventies, I did a rewrite Jimmy Webb's classic "Wichita Lineman." Here's the story: I worked at the Los Angeles Music Center as an usher. In those days, the Music Center had three performance venues and a wide variety of musicians played there. It was a great place to see everybody from Aretha Franklin to Maurice Chevalier. One of my favorite experiences was hearing Jerry Lee Lewis performing as Iago in Catch My Soul, a rock musical based on Shakespeare's Othello.

My best friend—then and now—is Arnie Zepel, a fellow usher at the time. Every year the ushers would have a talent contest and this particular year he wanted to win it because a girl he wanted to impress was on the committee. Arnie, while a great guy, was not exactly a strong singer or dancer, so I had to come up with something to make him shine. My answer was to write a parody to "Wichita Lineman," which I retitled "Music Center Usher."

Instead of "I am a lineman for the county, and I work the main road," I wrote, "I am an usher for the county, and I work the main floor." I filled the *lyrics with inside jokes that only an usher would get, and Arnie's charming delivery and my spot-on lyrics won the talent contest and cinched him a date with the girl.*

A *parody* is rewriting an existing song's lyrics for deliberate comic effect. Parodies are protected by the First Amendment of the U.S. Constitution. However, since parodies are based on the original lyric of the song, parodists depend on the "fair use" exception to combat claims of copyright infringement. Fair use is a U.S. law that permits limited use of copyrighted material without having to first acquire permission from the writer/publishers. Weird Al Yankovic is a master at parodies, and he's also very successful; he's had a number one album for each of the last five decades. Randy Rainbow, of YouTube fame, is another master of the genre. I've written parodies many times and find that adhering to the structure and rhyme scheme of a tune is a great tool to learn to write.

SONGWRITING ACTIONS

Now, back to "Penny Lane." Here's what you need to do:

Rewrite the lyrics to "Penny Lane," but keep the melody exactly the same. Retitle the song with another three-syllable location that had meaning for you as a child, like "Baldwin Hills," "Omaha," or "Sherman Oaks." Be sure to match the *stress* of the words "Penny Lane," which is on the first syllable. For example, the New Jersey town of Bridgewater has three syllables, but the stress is wrong. You can tell by trying to sing the word "Bridgewater" to the melody that goes with the words "Penny Lane" in the song. If you want a New Jersey town for your song, try "Basking Ridge." Sing it and you'll hear why.

1. Rewrite the vignettes in each verse of the song using scenes and characters from your childhood. For most writers, writing about your childhood can be a great way to access your emotions and the details only you know.

   - Keep The Beatles' *scansion* (length and rhythm of line) and rhyme scheme. It's critical to memorize the melody exactly, which means literally playing the tunes over and over until you learn it.
   - In the first verse, lines two, three, and four rhyme.

- In the second verse, lines two and three rhyme and then on line four, there's an inner rhyme (where the word in the middle of the line rhymes with the end word).
- In the chorus, lines one and two rhyme and line three doesn't.

OBJECTIVES OF SONGWRITING ACTIONS

To learn how to write lyrics that match the melody of the song. When the lyrics match the melody, it is called prosody. Make sure you can match The Beatles' melody in cadence and stress.

Learning to put your lyrics to a melody is a necessary ingredient in songwriting. Even if you have written the lyrics and the music together during the first verse, when you get to the second verse, you have to write different lyrics to the melody you have already set up. Memorizing the melody of the tune is ultimately much easier than thinking you're matching the lyrics to the melody by counting up the syllables and notating what syllables get stressed. Only by singing the words to the melody will you know if they work as a unit. It's a muscle you need to develop that will get better with time. Also, knowing the melody immediately gets you to sing and make what you are doing "musical" and not an abstract exercise on paper.

If you are a lyricist, you do not need to be a good singer, but singing the tune will let you know a multiplicity of things about the interplay between the words and the music. A songwriter friend of mine says that until you "taste" the words in your mouth you don't know if they work or not.

To make sure you have enough "specificity" in your song. Study The Beatles' lyric. The vignettes in each verse are like little movies and the nouns and verbs are specific: a banker and a barber and a fireman, not just a guy, another man, and a girl. In Nashville, songwriters call nouns and verbs that are very specific the "furniture." The more furniture the better.

To find the lyric for The Beatles' "Penny Lane," copy this link: https://tinyurl.com/2jdxztnk

As follows is one of my student's, Heather Perram Frank, rewrites of "Penny Lane." I picked her lyric because it has excellent furniture—specific nouns and verbs. It also has a consistent overall tone (a lazy summer vibe), location (East Coast), socioeconomic strata (upper middle class), and point of view (smart yet nostalgic).

Heather matched the lyrics perfectly to The Beatles' melody and kept to their rhyme scheme. She didn't approximate or paraphrase the melody but knew exactly the length and stresses in the song.

"Vicky Beach"
Parody Lyrics by Heather Perram Frank (Used with Permission)

Verse #1
On Vicky Beach there is a baby in a bouncy chair,
And all the moms are sitting smoking in the shade,
   Winkler: You can see the image and "smoking in the shade" is alliterative
Watching toddlers while they learn to wade.
   "Toddlers" is a cool word, nice specificity
It's thirty centigrade.

Verse #2
In the village there's a bakery and general store,
   Nice specifics
We ride our bikes and park them neatly in a rack,
   The next three lines are very visual and paint a nice scene of the village
We put our sugar cookies in a sack
And ride back again, very fast.

Chorus #1
Summer days have never been so sweet and slow,
   Alliteration again "summer," "sweet," and "slow"
Nothing much to do, nowhere to go,
But play and eat ice pops.
   Love the specific

I liked how Heather handled this assignment, so I told her to take the extra step and make this song its own entity. All that she needed to do was change the chorus, giving it a new scansion and rhyme scheme. Here's her transformed lyric that is now ready for a new melody to be put to it. Once she starts working with a composer, she may have to tinker a little further with the verse/rhyme scheme, depending on the new melody. Through the years, I have written a new set of lyrics to many hit songs, and even without tinkering with some of them, when I presented them my lyric, the composer never knew.

"Summer Days"
Parody Lyrics by Heather Perram Frank (Used with Permission)

Verse #1
On summer days there is a baby in a bouncy chair,
And all the mums are sitting smoking in the shade,
Watching toddlers while they learn to wade.
It's thirty centigrade.

Verse #2
In the village there's a bakery and a general store.
We ride our bikes and park them neatly in a rack.
We put our sugar cookies in a sack,
And ride back again, very fast.

Chorus #1
Summer days,
Summer days.
Have never been so sweet and slow.
Not much to tell, not much to know;
Nothing much to do, nowhere to go.
Summer days,
Summer days.

Here's another "Penny Lane" rewrite that I really like by my student Kilbourne Craddock. As with the previous rewrite and The Beatles original, Kilbourne creates a whole world for his song to live in. It's obviously set in Paris and the "furniture" supports that; for, lines like "the day begins at the boulangerie" take us immediately to Paris.

I also appreciate the breezy tone of the lines, and some of the humor. There's sophistication about the song that almost places it into the world of cabaret or musical theater.

REWRITING THE BEATLES, AND OTHER THINGS

Also, importantly, Kilbourne follows the melody of The Beatles tune perfectly. He catches each syllable of the tune as well as each stress and does it with a Parisian flair!

"Rue Madame"
Parody Lyrics by Kilbourne Craddock (Used with Permission)

Verse #1
On Rue Madame, the day begins at the boulangerie.
   Winkler: Immediately the location is set and it's French
The smells of croissants and espresso fill the air,
   Nice detail here
And Mademoiselle Béchaud sweeps the stair,
   Specific and alliterative
Curlers in her hair.
   Sometimes one thing can say so much

Verse #2
On the sidewalk flower stalls are full of daffodils;
   This verse is like watching a movie
The pretty ladies patronize a chic boutique.
   Alliteration is always nice—good detail and it's got an inner rhyme "chic" and "boutique"
A tourist gets directions from a flic,
   Charming—a French policeman
Happens ev'ry week—magnifique!
   Love this rhyme

Chorus #1
Rue Madame is just as Paris as you please,
   Cute phrase and alliterative
Shaded by the budding chestnut trees,
You're making memories
   Nice furniture

SONGWRITING ACTIONS

If you want one more music master from which to learn, Jimmy Webb is a great choice. He has written a lot of iconic songs such as "By the Time I Get to Phoenix," "Wichita Lineman," "MacArthur Park," and "Didn't We." One of my favorite songs of his, and to my knowledge the only hit song ever written about reincarnation (other than, perhaps, "Where or When") is the "The Highwayman." It was a *Billboard* number one country song and the 1986 Country Song of the Year at the GRAMMYS. It also was performed by a country supergroup—The Highwaymen, comprised of Johnny Cash, Willie Nelson, Waylon Jennings, and Kris Kristofferson.

The form of the song is just a series of "A"s, the traditional folk form used by Bob Dylan, Pete Seeger, and Joan Baez. Each "A" is a different incarnation—the first narrator is a highwayman, followed by a sailor, a dam builder, and the captain of a spaceship. The rhyme scheme is as follows: lines 2 and 3 rhyme, lines 4 and 5 rhyme and lines 6 and 7 rhyme.

> *You can find the lyric to "The Highwayman" at*
> *http://www.songlyrics.com/jimmy-webb/the-highwayman-lyrics/*

In 2019, another supergroup was formed, comprised of Brandi Carlisle, Maren Morris, Amanda Shires, and Natalie Hemby. They called themselves "The Highwomen," inspired by the Jimmy Webb song. The group released a *Billboard* number one country album, and their first single was a rewrite of "The Highwayman," in which they changed the narrator to a woman and her reincarnated lives as a highwoman, healer, preacher, freedom rider, and daughter. They contacted Jimmy Webb for his approval, which he gave wholeheartedly.

> *You can find the lyric to "The Highwomen" at:*
> *https://genius.com/The-highwomen-highwomen-lyrics*

So, your bonus assignment is to write a new lyric to the Jimmy Webb melody like "The Highwomen" did. You can change the narrators to famous singers through the years, famous visual artists, or even cars or buildings that have meaning for you. Be sure to keep Jimmy Webb's rhyme scheme and include a lot of "furniture" in your "A"s.

REWRITING THE BEATLES, AND OTHER THINGS

One of my students, Richard Castle, rewrote "The Highwayman." He's a musical theater writer who took my masters class. This is a class where more experienced writers share their songs weekly to get feedback led by me, with additional feedback by the other writers in the room. He has had quite a few of his musicals performed around the country. He has a lot of specifics in each "A" section and actually creates a whole world in each "A." His lyrics also adhere to the melody perfectly—no paraphrasing for him.

His song is about the legacy of men in positions of power who have bred hate, division, and abuse throughout history, ending with the modern equivalent of them on the internet. He uses the "craft" of songwriting to communicate his very relevant message for today.

These lines are very different from the ones in the charming Parisian song I quoted above; these are meant to disturb and provoke us, and it's the specificity that does it. We know that the writer is educated enough to know these details, and skillful enough so that we, as an audience, will immediately understand his message.

"The Strongmen"
Parody Lyrics by Richard Castle (Used with Permission)

A #2
I was a chancellor,
I rid Rhineland of the Jews.
Sold their hair and stole their shoes,
   Winkler: Such strong and disturbing specificity
I used my rallies to inflame and to provoke.
No one asked about the trains or of the smoke.
   Great detail
And in the end what if I too, was set aflame?
I'm not the one to blame.

A #4
I am a student,
I can't wait till I'm a man,
I'll join the skinheads or the Klan.
I hear the whistles calling out to me online,

I study guys like me who came before my time.
> *Once again strong specificity*

And with your silence I'll grow strong like all those men,
> *The alliteration of "silence" and strong" make the line have a real punch*

I'll be one of them,
You let us rise again and again and again,
And again, and again.

My student Sue Fleg does a different take than Richard Castle on the reincarnation theme of the song. Closer in spirit to the Jimmy Webb lyric, but from a female perspective.

"Life After Life"
Parody Lyrics by Sue Fleg (Used with Permission)

A#1
I was a courtesan—upon my beauty I relied
To Lords my favors I supplied
> *Winkler: I like the associative word "Lords," it fits the time period*

Many a traveler warmed his body by my flame
> *A nice way of saying it*

Many a young man knew my passion—not my name
A vengeful suitor took my life at thirty-five
But I am still alive

A#2
I was a dancer—I belonged upon the stage
A ballerina for the age
I skimmed the dance floor like a whirlwind hurricane
> *Nice imagery*

I was alight with the divine and the profane
And then one night, aloft—I leapt and fell—got killed . . .
But I am living still

9
RHYMING

I love to rhyme. So does Paul Simon. That's why he named one of his albums *There Goes Rhymin' Simon*.

Nothing makes me happier than to come up with an unexpected rhyme in a new song, a rhyme that moves my story along and surprises the listener. But I've found that sometimes new songwriters—especially those with a rebellious streak (you know who you are)—tell me they don't want to rhyme. My honest take is that the reason they don't want to rhyme is because good rhyming is just not that easy. Everyone can rhyme "you" with "do" or "night" with "right," but learning how to create unexpected wordplay, and to exploit the story of the song with your rhymes, takes more experience and ingenuity, and plain hard work. However, I promise you that it's worth your time and effort.

First of all, this is what rhymes do for your song:

- A variety of them (you'll get to this further down) make the song more interesting
- They can point the listener to important points in the story
- They can move the song along
- They can act as little hooks along the way, almost as a form of repetition
- They give the song structure: the rhyme scheme actually makes a listener unconsciously wait for the next rhyme (building tension) and when it comes, delivers a sweet release

That's a lot of bang for your buck! That's why 99 percent of all songs use rhyming. So, don't be scared—just jump in—and remember, learning to rhyme is a process (like learning to drive stick shift for the first time). When you first start, there are so many little details to remember. However, after a while, it becomes something you don't even think about—like second nature.

Different Kinds of Rhymes

- "Masculine rhymes" or "one rhymes" match the last syllable of a word at the end of a line with its rhyming partner.
  - Examples include "Stick, slick, kick, tick, lick" (I've always loved "ick" rhymes).

- "Feminine rhymes" or "double rhymes" match the next to the last syllable of a word at the end of a line with its rhyming partner.
  - Examples include "feather," "weather," "heather"; "tassel," "castle," "hassle."
  - When you want a double rhyme, start with a two-syllable word and then rhyme it.

- "Three rhymes" or "triple rhymes" include "history," "mystery," "misery." Or how about "kissing me," "missing me," "dissing me"? It doesn't have to be just one word, as long as you go two syllables back to make the rhyme.
  - When you want a triple rhyme, start with a three-syllable word and then rhyme it.

- "Four rhyme" is where you go three syllables back from the word or words at the end of the line to match it with its rhyming partner.
  - In "Sugar" by Maroon 5, the song has two examples of 4 rhymes
  - "*need*ing your love" paired with "*deep in* your love"
  - "Cuz I really *care* where you are" paired with "I just wanna be *there* where you are"
  - My favorite four rhyme in any song is from the great Julie London's 1955 rendition of "Cry Me a River" by Arthur Hamilton: "Told me love was *too* plebeian" paired with "Told me you were *through* with me and"

Winkler digresses . . .

The two lines I just singled out for praise stopped Arthur Hamilton, the songwriter of "Cry Me a River," from getting it into a big movie where it would be sung by one of the greatest singers of all time, Ella Fitzgerald. The movie was Pete Kelly's Blues *and the producers loved the song, they just wanted Arthur to replace the word "plebeian" with something a little less fancy, but Arthur said no. I think he realized he'd written a standard and that "plebeian" was the perfect word to describe the story at that moment in the song.*

It wasn't until Julie London, then a relatively unknown singer, wanted to sing it that it was recorded. Once again, the powers that be objected to the word "plebeian," which means "common," but Julie, who had been friends with Arthur in high school, stuck to her guns and the rest is history.

And two little known facts: Ella did eventually record "Cry Me a River" and it's a great rendition, and Arthur Hamilton was one of my songwriting teachers and a lovely man.

- "Perfect rhyme" is when the rhyming words have the same vowel and ending consonant sound, but with a different consonant sound on the beginning of the stressed syllable. Examples are "shout," "spout," "doubt." Also, "spender," "tender," "fender."
- "Imperfect rhyme" (also called a "slant" or "false rhyme") means that the rhyming words have either a different vowel or consonant (just one), with a different consonant sound on the beginning of the stressed syllable.
    - To say it another way, there has to be a difference in the rhyme: vowels rhyme, but consonants differ; vowels differ, but consonants are the same. For example, "world," "girl," is an imperfect rhyme because there is a "d" on the end of "world," which is an extra consonant from the "l" at the end of "girl." "Time," "mine" is an imperfect rhyme because the "m" in "time" is different than the "n" in "mine."

Winkler digresses . . .

Perfect rhyming is one of the hallmarks of the Great American Songbook, the term for the predominant popular music of the first half of the twentieth century. It's the music Frank Sinatra sang, written by such great composers as George and Ira Gershwin, Cole Porter, Richard Rodgers and Lorenz Hart. Lyricists in those days were masters of rhyming. However, as I mentioned before, things changed when rock and roll came along with its fresh and edgy "imperfect rhyme."

When I first started writing for musical theater in 1998, I came to my first show as a pop writer who didn't think anything of mixing perfect with imperfect rhyming.

I wrote songs for a little show called Naked Boys Singing!, which has played for over twenty years Off Broadway and is the second longest running show in Off Broadway history. In the show, there's a song called "Robert Mitchum," for which I wrote the lyrics.

"Robert Mitchum,"
Lyrics by Mark Winkler

As for me, I long for the days of
Robert Mitchum,
I know he was a little beefy and soft,
But when he took it all off,
He was bitchin'.

I rhymed "Mitchum" with "bitchin'" and the "um" and "in" consonants made the rhyme pairing imperfect—but it always got a big laugh from the audiences in the theater. Everyone loved it, except for a critic at *The Washington Post* who, though he liked the song, called out my "lazy rhyming in not coming up with a better rhyme for 'Mitchum.'" There's nothing like seeing your little song criticized in black and white to send shivers down your spine. However, since that time, with the advent of *Wicked*, *Hamilton*, and *Hadestown*, imperfect rhyming has become even more accepted on Broadway.

Winkler digresses even further . . . (whoa, Mark!)

As you may remember from the introduction, Randy Newman is one of my favorite songwriters. He is a lot more than "Short People" or "I Love L.A." or "You've Got a Friend in Me." The catalogue of his fifty years of songwriting is breathtaking. Check it out.

In the 1990s, Randy decided to write a musical called Faust, that was performed in La Jolla, California. It yielded the beautiful standard, "Feels Like Home" but didn't make it to Broadway. Somewhere in its journey, however, *the great lyricist and composer Stephen Sondheim and Randy met up and their exchange as reported in* The Los Angeles Times *went like this:*

Randy saw Mr. Sondheim and cheekily said: "I hope it doesn't offend you if I rhyme girl and world and things like that." Mr. Sondheim then said, "Well, it does bother me. I don't come from that tradition, and neither do you." And Randy said, "Oh, yes I do."

Randy went on to say that he grew up in rock and roll. "I loved Fats Domino, who rhymed New Orleans with shoes." Take that, Mr. Sondheim!

Rhyming in Rap

Rap, a major component of hip-hop, has been around for more than fifty years and its influences have permeated every genre of music. From pop records with rappers guesting—almost a prerequisite these days, to Nelly singing with Florida Georgia Line and Kane Brown using rap-inflected phrasing in country music, to the most successful musical of the last twenty years—Lin-Manuel Miranda's *Hamilton*—rap is everywhere.

Rhythm and rhyme are the two main components in rap. Melody is almost nonexistent or used only in certain places in the song, such as in a sample, a hook, or in a sung chorus. However, *rhyme* has a very significant role to play. Rhyming is so integral to rap, that it's as complicated, sophisticated, and omnipresent as rhyme used in musical theater. The major difference between the two is that the language used in rap is more urban street language and speaks in a vernacular that comes from the hip-hop world. Also, rhyme in rap uses predominately imperfect or slant rhymes. Which makes sense, because as I've said before, imperfect rhymes have been the preferred way to rhyme in pop, country, and, later, hip-hop music since the fifties. An example of imperfect rhyming is "nope" and "stroke." The vowels match, but the consonants differ.

Masculine (one rhymes), *feminine* (double rhymes), and *triple* rhymes are used extensively in rap.

Double rhymes are especially favored in rap. Some examples: in "Half Time" by Nas, he rhymes "mic back," "strike back," and "hype track." Pretty clever. Eminem has a great line in his song "Stay Wide Awake," which has three double rhymes in a row.

"Soon as my *flow starts*, I com*pose art* like the ghost of *Mozart*."

Speaking of "flow," "flow" is very important in rap. It is how the words land on the beat. The stress of the particular word will set up the rhythm pattern the rapper is using in the song. Their playground is in a four-beat bar. So, where they place the stresses and end the line will create the rhythm pattern. For example, if the rapper has a double rhyme on "four and," to keep the particular rhythm going, they keep ending the double rhyme on "four and." Then, when the rapper wants to change the flow, they'll change-up the rhyme by doing a three rhyme on "and four and," which is three syllables back from the end of the line.

Or they can do what Eminem did in "Stay Wide Awake" and do an internal rhyme, which is rhyming in the middle of the line "compose art" to the end of the line "ghost of Mozart." Internal rhyme has the effect on the listener of speeding up the line, creating tension, and showing off the rapper's dexterity and skill. The secret of a good flow is to keep doing these interesting rhyming choices, while sounding natural and smooth.

A great example of this is in "Low Down, Dirty" by Eminem.

"It was predicted by a *medic*, I'd grow up to be an addicted dia*betic*, living off liquid Tria*minic*, pa*thetic*." Wow!

Another technique rappers use is "bending words," using a word they have made up that will complete the rhyme.

There's an example in a song from J. Cole called "Immortal" where he rhymed the word "anyway" with "Virgini-A."

Or here's a fun one from Eminem in his song "Tone Deaf." "I can make an orange rhyme with ba*nana*, ora*nana*.

This immediately made me think of Yip Harburg, the great lyricist of *The Wizard of Oz* and *Finian's Rainbow*, who loved to "bend words." In "If I Were King of the Forest," the song the Lion sings in *The Wizard of Oz*, he wrote:

"though my tail would *lash*, I would show *compash*."

In rap, words are king, and rhyming, bending, flowing, and playing with words are the hallmarks of a great rapper. In pop, EDM, and R&B, "hooks" are of the utmost importance, and sometimes the lyrics are not as important as the melody and "ear worms" that these genres live on. In rap, a compelling story told in an authentic voice is what matters.

RHYMING

Winkler Digresses

Amazingly, in certain circles—mainly musical theater and cabaret—the battle still goes on between people who use imperfect/slant rhymes and "rhyme purists," but this is what I think: as much as I love perfect rhyming and craft, it's what you have to say that's the most important thing in a song. And if saying it "imperfectly" is the best way to say it, I'm fine with it. However, I do think perfect rhyming in comedy songs does get bigger laughs. That crazy micro of a microsecond that it takes for your brain to process an imperfect rhyme sometimes gets in the way of the laugh.

So, how do you go about rhyming when you've decided that you want to rhyme a word in your song. Take a sentence and then rhyme it, for example, this is from my song "Future Street":

Right there at the intersection
Of satisfaction and *complete*,
Gonna live my dreams _ _ _ _ *(four syllables leading to rhyme)*

The word I'm rhyming is "complete." I use two methods: my first is a rhyming dictionary. I'm old-school and still use my old paperback *Capricorn Rhyming Dictionary*. Stephen Sondheim used Clement Wood's *The Complete Rhyming Dictionary*. Of course, most people go to the internet for the rhymes. A couple of other places to go are rhymer.com or rhymezone.com. When I go to my trusty rhyming dictionary, I'm in luck, for there are many rhymes for *complete* like "seat," "feet," and "sweet." I wind up using *street*.

Right there at the intersection
Of satisfaction and *complete*,
Gonna live my dreams on future *street*.

Another method I use is very organic. I take the word "complete" and literally use my fingers to count up the alphabet until I find a rhyme I like—a, b, c, d, to z. It works for me; I've been doing it forever. So, if I'm starting with trying to rhyme "complete"—"beat," "creep," "deep," "feet" are my rhymes going down the alphabet.

Schemes

Rhyme schemes in a song create structure and cohesion. They can emphasize your story and add variety too.

So, if you think of each verse as four lines, a typical rhyme scheme would be: ABAB—every other line.

There's also AABA—the first two lines rhyme, then the second two lines rhyme. And AAAA, in which every line rhymes.

In a perfect songwriting world, the rhyme scheme you set up in the first verse is carried through in your other verses. And you'll want a different rhyme scheme in your chorus and your bridge.

"Inner rhyming" occurs within a single line, when a word in the middle of the line rhymes with the end word of the line. For example, here's inner rhyme from "Don't Stop Believin'" by Journey:

A singer in a smokey *room*,
The smell of wine and cheap *perfume*

Or in The Beatles' "A Hard Day's Night"

But when I come home to *you*, I find the things that you *do*
Will make me feel alright.

Final Thoughts on Rhyming.

I have found that the best rhymes occur when two words that are most unlike each other are rhymed. Such as, "Let me" and "Chevy"—or "paper" and "satyr" are good; "can" and "and" are rather boring.

An interesting choice of word leads to a unique rhyme; the unique rhyme leads to an extraordinary word.

Songwriting Actions

Print out the lyrics of three of your favorite hit songs and identify the different types of rhymes and note whether they are perfect or imperfect. In doing this, you'll have an even greater pleasure listening to the songs because you'll appreciate the craft that went into creating them.

10
LAUNDRY LIST SONGS

Making a list, checking it twice . . .

Since the earliest days of songwriting, the successful technique of using a "laundry list" is a stimulating way to write a tune, and it can give your lyrics a lot of specificity and impact. Lists of things provide plenty of adjectives, nouns, and verbs, all of which are perfect material for "furniture."

A laundry list song (also called a "list song" or "catalogue" song) is usually developed by literally writing a list of words and phrases connected to the story you want to tell. In musical theater and in country music, the list song is often humorous. Frequently, each new section of the song serves to escalate the absurdity.

The lyrics of my favorite list song, written by Arthur Schwartz (who also wrote "Haunted Heart," "Alone Together," and "Dancing in the Dark," among others) uses a list of U.S. state names and their famous products to illustrate a love song dedicated to a girl from Rhode Island. By the last "A" section of the song, the products become totally wacky—"Pencils from Pencil-vania" and "Vests from Vest Virginia"; the hook (and the title) is "Rhode Island Is Famous for You." Originally written for an obscure Broadway musical revue, *Inside U.S.A.*, the song has been sung by Blossom Dearie, Alice Faye, John Pizzarelli, and yours truly, on my album with Cheryl Bentyne, *Eastern Standard Time*.

The laundry list technique can be used throughout a tune, or in any part of the tune. It's only used in the chorus of Tim McGraw's hit "Live Like You're Dying," written by Tim Nichols and Craig Wiseman (Song of the Year at the GRAMMYS and the biggest country tune of 2004). The entire lyric of "My Favorite Things" from Rodgers and Hammerstein II's *The Sound of Music* is a laundry list. In Lorde's 2013 smash, "Royals" (written with Joel Little), it's just in the pre-chorus.

Winkler digresses:
Laundry list songs are my favorite things in the world to write. I have written many, and truthfully, I have to stop myself from writing them. But if you're having problems coming up with a song idea, use the laundry list technique and your life will suddenly be a whole lot easier.

Once, while I was driving my car and listening to "The Highway" on Sirius XM, three laundry list songs came on, one after another. First there was Morgan Wallen's "More Than My Hometown," then Thomas Rhett's "What's Your Country Song?," and then the classic Lee Ann Womack song, "I Hope You Dance" (a wedding song fave since its release in 2000). Written by Mark D. Sanders and Tia Siller, "I Hope You Dance" topped the country charts, went to number 14 on the pop charts and, you guessed it, won the GRAMMY Award for Best County Song of the Year. Country music, with its appreciation for craft and technique, loves the list song.

Here's a diverse list of songs that use the laundry list technique:

Country
"Before He Cheats" by Carrie Underwood
"Female" by Keith Urban
"Redneck Woman" by Gretchen Wilson

Disney Classics
"The Bare Necessities" from *The Jungle Book*
"Under the Sea" from *The Little Mermaid*

Folk-Rock
"Blowin' in the Wind," "Forever Young," and "Serve Somebody" by Bob Dylan

Jazz
"Better Than Anything" by David Wheat and Bill Loughborough
"I'm Hip" by Bob Dorough and Dave Frishberg

Musical Theater
"Anything Goes," "It's DeLovely," "You're the Top," from *Anything Goes*; "Brush Up Your Shakespeare," from *Kiss Me Kate* by Cole Porter
"Mix Tape" from *Avenue Q* by Robert Lopez and Jeff Marx
"Seasons of Love" from *Rent* by Jonathan Larson
"It Takes Two" from *Hairspray* by Mark Shaiman and Scott Whitman

Pop
"If I Were a Boy" by Beyoncé
"Last Friday Night" by Katy Perry
"New Rules" by Dua Lipa
"The Lazy Song" and "That's What I Like" by Bruno Mars
"We Didn't Start the Fire" by Billy Joel

R&B/Soul/Hip-Hop/Rap
"Wonderful World" by Sam Cooke
"Dancing in the Streets" recorded by Martha and the Vandellas
"Empire State of Mind" by Alicia Keys
"99 Problems" by Jay-Z
"The Message" by Grandmaster Flash

SONGWRITING ACTIONS
Your choice. Pick one:

1. Write new lyrics for the list of things that Katy Perry can't remember, but wakes up to, in the verses of "Last Friday Night," matching the song's original melody. The rhyme scheme is as follows: In the verse, rhyme lines 1 and 2; 3 and 4; 5 and 6; 7 and 8. In the chorus, rhyme lines 2, 3, and 4, but no need to rewrite the second half of the chorus.
2. Write new lyrics for the "bucket list" chorus of Tim McGraw's "Live Like You Were Dying," matching the song's original melody. Keep the song title but substitute a new list of things. The rhyme scheme is as follows:

lines 1 and 2 rhyme (both double rhymes: DIving with CLImbing); lines 4 and 5 rhyme (both double rhymes: DEEper and SWEEter); line 6 rhymes with line 2 (both double rhymes: deNYing and CLImbing); and line 9 rhymes with line 6 (both double rhymes: DYing and deNYing).
3. Write the first "A" section of Cole Porter's "You're the Top," matching the song's original melody. Keep the song title but substitute a new list of things. Keep Porter's rhyme scheme (which is complicated). In the first "A" section, rhyme lines 2 and 4 (both double rhymes: coliSEum with muSEum); then an inner-rhyme in line 5 (both are three rhymes: MElody with SYMphony). Lines 6 and 7 are double rhymes: BONnet with SONnet. In line 8 (a one rhyme), MOUSE rhymes with line 5's STRAUSS.
4. Rewrite the jazz classic "Better Than Anything." Rhyme lines 2 and 4; 6 and 8; then 9 and 10 in the long "A."

Winkler digresses:
I've been teaching my students to rewrite "Better Than Anything" for a long time.

Here are some versions of "Better Than Anything" by a few talented students of mine. One of them is David Puretz, who took the laundry list of the song in a definite jazz direction. All of my students' lyrics that I'm featuring are full of "furniture" and clever wordplay.

"Better Than Anything"
Parody lyrics by David Puretz (Used with Permission)

Better than Nina at Newport,
Better than Milt at Montreux,
Better than Sassy's Vaughn's retort,
Better than Monk's piano.
Better than Duke's "Take the 'A' Train,"
Better than Miles blowin' hard,
Better than groovin' with Coltrane
At the Village Vanguard.
Better than Dave Brubeck's work,
"Blue Rondo à la Turk"
Better than anything except being in love.

Better than Ella singing Gershwin,
Better than Dino clownin' drunk,
Better than Bing croonin' Berlin,
Better than Judy in a funk.
Better than Frank's "Doo Be Doo Be,"
Better than Wayne's "Danke Schoen,"
Better than dancin' by Sammy,
Better than Shirley MacLaine.
Better than Basie's Big Bands,
The Rat Pack at the Sands,
Better than anything except being in love.

Better than a great big hit song,
Better than jazz all night long,
Better than anything except being in love.

Here's an homage to Cole Porter's "You're the Top" by my student Mark Govatos. By the way, this song's tight structure, with different difficult rhymes, is a true challenge.

"You're the Top"
Parody Lyrics by Mark Govatos (Used with Permission)

You're the top,
You're a night in Paris.
You're the top,
You're a moonlit terrace.
You're a Christmas song I always love to sing,
You're a movie star,
You're caviar.
You're a diamond ring . . .
You're the dew
From a Roman fountain,
You're the view from the highest mountain,
I'm a rusty coin that people always drop,
But if, baby, I'm the bottom you're the top!

You're the top!
You're a cashmere sweater,
You're the top!
You're the perfect weather,
You're a game I play that I can never lose.
You're a winning bet,
A private jet,
A pleasure cruise . . .
You're a pearl,
You're a five-star rating,
You're the girl I dream of dating,
I'm the schmutz you see when wringing out a mop,
But if, baby, I'm the bottom you're the top!

11

TOP TEN TIPS FOR LYRIC WRITERS: TIPS 6-10

6. Use a dummy melody

If you're writing the lyric first, and have not been given a melody, come up with a dummy melody. I find this far better than writing lyrics with no melody. (When that is the case, many new songwriters seem to wind up counting the number of syllables in each line and putting in the stresses. But that's far too complicated.) Coming up with a dummy melody automatically gives you stresses—while naturally giving you "scansion" (the rhythm and length of the line). If your words don't match the melody, it's not correct. Easy.

On the songs for which I write the lyrics first, this is what I do:

I usually have a first verse or a first and second verse in place—four or eight lines—with a rhyme scheme in place as well. Then I literally begin pounding on my chest in the meter I want to write the lyric to (usually it's in four/four time), and I start singing. Here's the important thing to remember—the melody you come up with doesn't have to be good. Most of mine aren't. Its only function is to give you a melody, so when you get to the next verse, your lyrics will match in length and stresses. Then, when you sing the line, everything falls into place in a musical and natural way.

I know some of you may be shaking your heads and saying, "I'm not a singer" and/or "I don't want to sing." And I respond that some of my favorite melody writers aren't great singers either (Has anybody heard Burt Bacharach sing?), but making the lyrics "musical" from the get-go is a very wise thing to do. It makes what you are doing into a song immediately, which is what you're ultimately going for. It also shows you if some of the words or phrases you've come up with will roll off your tongue or collapse in a pitiful heap of bruised consonants. As my friend and top jazz singer Sinne Eeg told me over dinner, "When I write a song, I want the words to taste good in my mouth."

Another tactic is to find a great melody you like and put new words to it. There are plenty of reasons the song you like is a hit, so why not piggyback on it and use its excellent structure and rhyme schemes as the template for your song? You may find that it's better to pick a song where you don't really know the lyrics, except for a couple of phrases. It's easy to find karaoke versions of top hits and you can sing over the track while creating your song. Personally, I think this is a lot of fun and once again, it immediately makes your lyric musical and not just some words on paper. I've done this many times, and when I've shown the finished lyric to the melody writers I want to put a melody to my lyric, not one of them has made the connection. It works like a charm.

Winkler digresses . . .

I was cutting one of my jazz albums a few years ago and working with a brilliant pianist and composer on a well-known jazz standard. The only problem was that the pianist didn't make it easy for me as a singer to know where to come in and out of the song. He was so overly hip, sometimes I didn't know where I was at in the song, because during his instrumental, he never referenced the actual melody of the song. So, after the take, I asked this multiple-GRAMMY-winning guy if maybe he could play the melody a little more (note to aspiring jazz singers: never ask a jazz musician to play more melody) and he got mad and left the studio. Luckily, my producer, Barbara Brighton, is not only a consummate record producer but also a therapist by day. She gathered up the pianist and me and did a little intervention right there in the break room of the recording studio. Barbara quickly worked her magic, we communicated, and then headed back into the studio. He did play the song a little more conventionally, yet beautifully, and I nailed the vocal quite easily.

But here's the funny thing. Even though I had a hell of a time singing the first take, I thought it was beautiful and never forgot it. And a few years later,

I went to the studio and had them put the original track on a hard drive for me. When I listened to it, I almost immediately started "toplining" another melody and lyric to the track and it wound up being on my album Sweet Spot.

The name of the song I came up with is "This Side of Loving." When you hear it, try to guess the jazz standard that inspired the original recording! I'm not telling.

"Toplining" is a popular songwriting technique. It is widely used in the world of pop, hip-hop, and electronic dance music. The topliner gets a pre-made instrumental track and then comes up with both the melody and lyrics over the changes and arrangement they were presented with.

Through my students, I also learned that on YouTube, there are tracks and "feels" to songs in the style of just about every singer and genre you can think of. So, if you want to write a song in the style of Adele or Bruno Mars or Alicia Keys or Beyoncé, it's there at your fingertips. Plus, there are sites that have tracks you can use for a fee—two that come to mind are Writer Tracks and JustAddVocals.com.

7. Writing is rewriting

Ask any professional songwriter what separates them from an amateur and they'll say their ability to "rewrite," and to not settle for the first thing that pops into their mind.

The professional loves songs and songwriting. The amateur wants quick money and thinks that songwriting is an easy way to get it. They don't spend enough time on each song. They submit songs in their first draft. They don't go over them as painstakingly as professional writers do.

—*Oscar Hammerstein, II*

I had a friend who wrote a musical about Elon Musk. It was terrible—sloppy, amateurish, and sophomoric. To him, the great accomplishment was in writing twenty songs in seven days. They were appalling, with titles like "Twitter Man" and "Plug Me In (Start Me Up)." I dreaded having to tell him what I really thought. So, when he finally called me, all I could say was, "Wow, what an accomplishment—twenty songs in seven days!"

The truth is that it is definitely not the quantity of songs you write, but the quality. I've written over four hundred songs in my lifetime. I don't need to write another song, what I need to do is write a really good song.

Here's how I do it.

On the first pass, I always try to get as much of the song lyric down as I can by flinging out lines that stump me with any words that give me cadence and rhyme. This lets me map out the song in front of me. Then I put a little "x" in front of the lines that can be improved. I have a friend, Glenn Ballantyne, who was a staff writer at a major publisher and had a crazy quota of writing seventy-five songs a year. When I asked him how he did it, he said that when he wrote a song, he didn't let a bad line or two stop his flow. He'd write the lines down and then change them on the next pass.

So then, in an hour or two after you take a shower, or have a good night's rest, go back to the song. You'll see what you've got after the first intoxication of inspiration has worn off.

Remember that Paul McCartney's first pass on the lyrics to "Yesterday" (which he dreamed!) were, "Scrambled eggs, all I want is ham and scrambled eggs." I'm glad Paul didn't settle for the first thing that came to his mind.

I've had a few miracle wonders where the whole thing just came out perfectly on the first pass. Ninety-nine percent of the time, I've had to go back many times to change lines that bothered me.

You'll be glad you did—it's what lifts something good to very good or even great. And to answer your question "When do you know when it's finished?" It's when you make it as good as you possibly can, then play it to an audience or a publisher and receive an overwhelmingly positive response.

8. Once is never enough (hooks, hooks, hooks)

According to Leonard Bernstein, "The repetitive principle is at the very source of musical art and of poetry."

Sometimes when beginning songwriters bring in their work, I notice there is not enough repetition in their songs. When I ask them about it, they say they don't want to "sell out" or they want to "do their own thing." However, everyone from Cole Porter to Bruce Springsteen to Ed Sheeran understands that repeated elements in the song will hook the listener. Every well-conceived repetition not only pleases the ear, but also draws us in, lending order and structure to a song.

Common lyrical devices:

- *Repetition of the main hook* (usually the title or a phrase in the chorus): It's the part where, if you haven't finalized/determined the title of the song, you sing to your friend to see if they know it.
- *Repetition of nonsense/primarily musical phrases*: Called "vocables," they can be found anywhere in the song.
- *The return*: The reappearance of the first A section in an AABA song—such as heard in "Annie's Song" or "California Dreamin'," or the repetition of a verse in a verse/chorus song such as "Mr. Brightside," "Wonderwall," and "Can't Get You Out of My Mind."
- *The refrain*: In AABA form, such as "Nearness of You" or "The Way We Were," this is the main *hook* in an AABA song. And when you write it melodically, think of "stepping out the title." This means to make it special by not just using it as another line in the "A" of the song, but to play with the rhythm or range of it to make it "hookier" and more memorable.
- *Alliteration*: Starting each word or most words in the sentence with the same letter. This device makes it easier for the singer to sing the words and the repetition of sounds is pleasing to the ear, for example, "Bewitched, Bothered and Bewildered."
- *Anaphora*: An old speech-making device that means starting or ending two or more sentences of the tune with the same words. For example, "Imma Be," "According to You," "I Hope You Dance," "Miss Independence," "I Wish You Love."
- *Melodic or instrumental motifs that stand out*: Such as the horns in "Crazy in Love"; the broken piano chords at the top of "The Way We Were" and "Close to You"; and the guitar riff in "(I Can't Get No) Satisfaction."

Whenever you think you're repeating things too much, remember that Cole Porter repeats the title "You're the Top" three times in his first A section alone or think of a Black-Eyed Peas song.

Things don't change very fast in the world of songwriting, but something new has transpired in the last few years—the idea that instead of one or two hooks occurring in a pop song, there could be as many as seven or eight hooks and that each section contains a hook or hooks.

The first time I noticed this phenomenon is in Kylie Minogue's "Can't Get You Off of My Mind" single. It was as if every section featured another hook. Check it out on YouTube. will.i.am and the Black-Eyed Peas are masters of this, especially their "I Gotta Feeling," which includes:

- Title repetition to the max
- Phrase throwing (a line that in of itself is catchy, although may not mean that much)
- Call and response (like in church)
- Nonsense melodic phrases (vocables)
- Melodic/instrumental hooks
- Shout outs, like a list of days

9. Know your market

For many years, my day job was in movie market research. I literally "coded" people's comments about the movies, trailers, and commercials that the major movie studios put out. It taught me a lot about the public. It really shattered many of my artistic misconceptions. And there are a lot of similarities between movies and songs:

- They're both vying for the public's attention
- They both have dedicated audiences and infrequent audiences
- They both need good titles, a clear storyline, and things that hook their audience
- They follow set forms

Here are some misconceptions that artists have:

- *"There's nobody like me, I can't compare myself to anyone else."*
  First of all, I believe we are all unique, and these special qualities should be developed. It's what separates us from the pack. But most of us do fit into certain categories, and if you can't give somebody a description of what your song is like, they'll be more than happy to put it in a category for you.

  It's not a crime when somebody asks what you write—to say, "Top Forty pop like Justin Bieber or hip-hop/pop like Lizzo or jazzy songs like Diana Krall or country songs like Carrie Underwood."

- *"To be a big success, everyone must love my work."*
  Everybody won't love your work. When I was working at my market research job, we screened a little movie called *Forrest Gump* and its positive scores went through the roof. But guess what? There were people out there who hated *Forrest Gump*. Generally, it was the young males who thought *Pulp Fiction* (released in the same year) was the best thing they ever saw. And guess what? A segment of the public abhorred *Pulp Fiction*. Both movies were pop sensations and both movies grossed $400 million. You don't have to get everybody to like you. You just have to get *some* people to like you.

- *"People don't know what they like."*
  Oh, yes they do. People are quite clear about what they like. And they are only too willing to tell you. You just need to find the ones that like you!

Know your likely genre and fans will help you, because each kind of song has certain requirements. If you're writing a song for Britney Spears (if she's performing), it better have a good beat; the rhymes don't have to be perfect, but it has to have hooks and some cool musical ear candy (remember "Toxic"?). Whereas a song for Diana Krall should have clever lyrics, perfectly rhymed with sensuous overtones. Her audience is older and appreciates craftsmanship as found in the Great American Songbook.

What kind of songs do you write? As a songwriter you can write more than one kind. Diane Warren, one of the most successful popular songwriters of the last forty years, writes ballads, dance, country, rock, R&B, and movie themes, for instance:

Pop: "Because You Loved Me," performed by Celine Dion
Dance: "Can't Fight the Moonlight," performed by LeAnn Rimes, "Rhythm of the Night" performed by DeBarge
Rock: "I Don't Want to Miss a Thing," performed by Aerosmith
Country: "How Do I Live?" performed by LeAnn Rimes
Jazz: "Any Other Fool," performed by Patti Austin and Sadao Watanabe
Movie theme: "Why Did You Do That?" written for *A Star Is Born*

As a songwriter, you must listen to the radio, browse incessantly through YouTube and all the current social media, and check out your competition. If you want to be a pop writer, it's essential to listen to the station or streaming channels that would most likely play your song. If it's theater songs, you need to listen to the latest musicals. In the last two decades in musical theater, there has been a big shift away from the English sung-through musicals of Andrew Lloyd Webber to lighter pieces with a book like *Mean Girls*, *Beautiful*, and *Waitress* with imperfect rhymes and strong pop influences. And the blending of rap and pop in *Hamilton* was revolutionary in the theater. Music is constantly changing, which leads to my last tip . . .

10. What's not happening in music now? Do it.

Things change fast in music. But sometimes in the pop world, when styles go out of fashion, it takes quite a lot of time for them to come around again. Before Adele came along, the last ballad to be a pop hit on the charts was Faith Hill's 2001 "There You'll Be (Theme from *Pearl Harbor*)," written by Diane Warren. There were seven years between Faith Hill's ballad and Adele's "Chasing Pavement" ballad, which reached number 21 on the *Billboard* Pop Charts. And ten years between Faith's ballad and Adele's number 1 smash "Someone Like You." That's right, no ballads on the charts—a lot of midtempo, dance, and EDM crowding the Top Forty, though. However, after Adele won every GRAMMY in sight and became a superstar, suddenly ballads like Rihanna's "Diamonds" and Bruno Mars's "When I Was Your Man," were everywhere.

Meghan Trainor did the same thing with her 2014 smash "All About That Bass." Before her, the 1950s rhythm the song is based on hadn't been heard since "Grease" in the late seventies. Once she went to number 1 and was nominated for a GRAMMY for Song of the Year, she wisely had a couple more hits with that rhythm, took a break, and has started using it again, resulting in her 2022 smash "Made You Look." It definitely sets her apart.

Lady Gaga was in a little slump (Where do you go after a meat dress?) when she switched gears and went from dance/pop and Little Monsters to jazz and Tony Bennett and scored a big hit with their album *Cheek to Cheek*.

Savvy record producer David Foster saw a gap in pop music when he realized that there was nobody doing the Great American Songbook (think Frank Sinatra and Bobby Darin), so he found a young, handsome Canadian singer with killer chops, Michael Bublé, and produced a lot of platinum and gold records with him. Then, Foster took note of how popular Italian sensation Andrea Bocelli was becoming by mixing opera and romantic pop songs, so he introduced a young American singer with comparable abilities, Josh Groban, to do much of the same thing, but this time in English. These two genres hadn't been happening since Frank Sinatra and Mario Lanza, respectively. But in music, everything old is new again.

Consider what's not happening in music right now and make a list. Your list may not age well, because, as I've pointed out, what's out can suddenly be in again.

Here are mine:

- Comedy songs
- Songs in the AABA form
- Sax solos
- Instrumentals (songs with no lyrics)
- Perfect rhyming
- Songs based on hit foreign songs with English lyrics
- Folk songs with banjos
- Songs with trumpets and whistling
- Songs with backup singers

Putting some of these elements back into your songs where they feel organic and natural will definitely set you apart and may just start a trend. When I was chasing the next hit in my early days, I couldn't help but realize that publishers were always having us, the hungry and neophyte tunesmiths, chasing the hit and trend that had already happened. I think it's smarter to chase the hit or trend that *will* happen. Try it!

12

TROPICAL NIGHTS: ME 'N' LIZA!

My first song that was recorded was "Tropical Nights." The song was the result of an assignment in my songwriting class with Al Kasha where he brought in a book of *Vogue* magazine covers from the 1930s. In those days, the covers were illustrations, not photographs. The elaborate images featured glamorous women in exciting settings, reflecting the times and the art deco look of the era.

Kasha asked us to leaf through the book and pick an illustration that we could turn into a song. We needed to take the specific information in the picture, put it into the song, and use it to tell the story. I picked an illustration of an elegant lady dressed to the nines. She had a long cigarette holder, a cloche hat, and a sparkly shawl. She was definitely sophisticated and out for a good time. In the background was the ocean and a modern, streamlined ocean liner. In the sky above her head was the word "Vogue" spelled out in large stars.

It was the mid-seventies and there was a retro-nostalgia movement going on in music. Major recording artists were reviving the music of the 1930s and 1940s, such as "Boogie-Woogie Bugle Boy" with Bette Midler, "Java Jive" with the Manhattan Transfer, "Just a Gigolo" with Peter Allen (also David Lee Roth), and "Show Biz" by Helen Reddy. There was a *Billboard* number one song at the time called "Midnight at the Oasis" sung by Maria Muldaur, which was very much in this style, so I decided my song would also be a charming, thirties-inspired shuffle.

I wrote the song using all the elements of the *Vogue* magazine cover. It's about a guy trying to woo a sophisticated lady to fall in love with him. They're having a shipboard romance, and dancing under the stars on a tropical night.

"Tropical Nights"
Words and Music by Mark Winkler

Sophisticated someone
   Winkler: Obviously, the lady on the cover is not a working-class woman
Dressed in all of your finery;
   The lady was in a lovely dress on the cover
I wanna share all your smiles,
Linger a while 'neath a starry palm tree.
I know that we're just
A shipboard romance,
   There's a ship in the background on the magazine cover
But won't you take a chance.
Sophisticated someone,
Can I have this last dance?

Chorus
Tropical nights, tropical nights,
   The starry night and the ship led me to the conclusion they were in the tropics
Stars look big as diamonds,
   The title of the magazine is spelled out in large stars
And my head's feelin' light.
Tropical nights, tropical nights,
I hear my heart a-rockin',
Tellin' me that cupid's knockin'.

It was by far the best song I had written up to that point. One of my other songs was called "Love Stains" (hell, I was young!), so there wasn't a lot of competition.

Winkler digresses . . .

I learned something unexpectedly by lucking out and writing a good song as a fledgling songwriter. I would be in a publisher's office on Sunset pounding out one of my tunes on their upright, while they were talking on the phone, buffing their nails, or calling their secretaries to the room for an emergency conference. But the minute I played "Tropical Nights," all unnecessary activity ceased. The overly busy publishers suddenly stopped what they were doing and listened to me. That is the power of a good song.

I was working as a waiter at this crazy restaurant in Beverly Hills called the Chopping Block. Steve March-Tormé came in frequently. He is Mel Tormé's son and a very talented singer-songwriter in his own right. He had just released his first album on United Artists records and he knew that I sang and wrote songs too.

One day, he informed me that he was producing an album for Liza Minnelli and asked if I had any songs she might like. Steve and Liza had grown up in Hollywood together as offspring of famous parents. I thought "Tropical Nights," being an old-fashioned shuffle, was just the ticket for Liza. I recall making him a cassette (Remember those?) of the song and then not hearing anything back from him. Nothing unusual about that: in those days, with my three or four songs, I never heard anything back from anyone.

And then, one starry night, this musician friend of mine, Robby Robinson, called and said Liza Minnelli was doing my song "Tropical Nights" right that very minute, with a thirty-piece orchestra in Hollywood—and it was fabulous! So fabulous that it was going to be the title of her new album. Now, let me put this into context: Liza had just finished the movie New York, New York *and was one of the biggest stars on the planet. Meanwhile, I'm living in a one-room apartment in the hills above the Capitol Records building, an apartment so small that every night when I went to sleep, my head was just inches from the front door. Obviously, I was very excited!*

Later, I learned from my friend that they'd turned my little three-minute shuffle into a six-and-a-half-minute disco extravaganza with a rainstorm, a conga line, and the melody of "Bali Hai" opening it all up. Of course, "Bali Hai" was from the big Broadway hit by Rodgers & Hammerstein II, South Pacific, *and when the record did finally come out, the Columbia label read (Winkler/Rodgers/Hammerstein II). Really cool for a guy's first recording.*

Mark in front of his career poster wall with his Liza Minnelli Tropical Nights album cover (photo by Mark Winkler).

But in the tradition of Hollywood, I didn't hear anything back from Liza or Steve March-Tormé for two months. In the meantime, I had been working with a wonderful publisher, Don Blocker, who was starting up a new publishing company and needed some cuts immediately.

When I told him that Liza had just recorded my tune, he plopped five hundred dollars on the desk in front of me, and he said that I could have the money if I gave him half the publishing. Remember, at the time I was living on tuna casseroles and diet cokes, so faster than you can say "Bob Fosse," I took him up on the offer. Good thing I did, because the record label tried to get my publishing, saying they were "thinking" of putting my song on the album. We knew they'd already spent big bucks hiring ace photographer Reid Miles to create the whole world of tropical nights for the album cover, so we were not dissuaded. But it was nice to have some Hollywood muscle backing me up.

The album came out and it didn't set the world on fire, but it was a smash at Studio 54. And it was featured in an infamous "Oscar Night" special with Cheryl Ladd and Ben Vereen, that is like some crazy outtake from a "Village People meets Bob Fosse" video. You can watch it on YouTube.

Winkler digresses . . .
One of the nifty things about songwriting is you never know what the trajectory will be for a song. "Tropical Nights," because it was sung by such an icon as Liza, has had a great afterlife. Through the years, it has been featured in every drag bar from Studio City to Tokyo. There was a revue in Australia called "Tropical Nights" that featured it and ran for two years, and it was even performed as a ballet by a prestigious New York dance company!

So, let's take Al Kasha's assignment for me that resulted in "Tropical Nights," and use it as your next songwriting action.

SONGWRITING ACTIONS
Find a picture by googling a subject or an artist you like.

Through the years, my students have had good luck writing songs to the works of artists such as Van Gogh, Picasso, and Dali, and to photographs as well. The trick is to pick a picture that has elements you can put in a song—*location, people,* or something that involves *action.* Don't choose abstract pictures or images with few details.

Then, write a song about that picture using elements seen in it. Here's an example of a painting that inspired a song I wrote. I picked my favorite David Hockney painting called "Portrait of an Artist (Pool with Two Figures)" that sold recently for a record $90.3 million—one of the highest sums ever paid for a living artist. I wrote a song called "Beguiled" that is on my album *Tales From Hollywood.* Here's the first verse:

I watch your body,
Swimming through the pool,
Pushing off the sidewall,
Tan against blue.

Using the actual elements in the picture—the pool, the blue and tan coloring, the person swimming—I basically just described the scene.

Below are lyrics based on pictures that my students wrote for the class.

This is a lyric my student Shelley Nyman wrote to "Nighthawks" by Edward Hopper. She did a wonderful job of taking the characters at the diner, the mood of the painting, and even the diner's sign and putting it in the tune.

"Phillies 5-cent Cigars"
Lyrics by Shelley Nyman (Used with Permission)

And there 'round the corner, I saw the café,
Open for 24 hours a day.
   Winkler: The café being open twenty-four hours taken from the painting
And the glaring fluorescents inside lit my way . . . through the door,
   Once again, the bright lighting is taken from the painting
And the sign said, "Phillies Cigars, 5-cent, Phillies Cigars."
   Ad from above the café window in the painting.

I sat at the counter, the coffee was strong,
   The counter and drinking coffee taken from the painting
And nobody asked me, "Hey, buddy what's wrong?"

I knew I could wait there 'til night turned to dawn . . . so I would, if I could.

A red-headed woman . . . stared at her hand;
   The woman staring at her hand taken from the painting
The waiter in white looked too tired to stand;
   The waiter in white and his slumped posture is taken from the painting
A nose like a hawk on a vacant-eyed man.
   The guy in the hat at the counter is described well
He looked lost . . . like me
And the sign said, "Phillies Cigars, 5-cent, Phillies Cigars."
   Taken directly from the painting

This next song is based on the painting "Plum Brandy" by Edouard Manet. Once again, the writer, Heather Perram Frank, captures beautifully the elegance and loneliness of the lady sitting at a table for one. There's less specific detail from the painting in this one. Rather, the painting is used as a means to set up a situation where the lyricist can use her imagination to create a whole scene as if in a movie. Franks also delivers an incredibly sophisticated lyric.

"Just One"
Lyrics by Heather Perram Frank (Used with Permission)

"How many?" asks the hostess with a dazzling smile,
"Just one," I say, as she leads me away,
I wonder as we pass the tables if I look okay,
"No one's looking at you anyway," to myself I say.

The woman to my left is fiddling with her wine,
She's overdressed for both the time and place.
Her haircut calls attention to the deep lines in her face,
She asks her companion, "What about the lace?"

Just one,
I know,
Doesn't sound like much fun.

Just one,
Only me,
In a world of twos,
Without you.

I order the short ribs, the ones you loved so much,
With the sauce that always made you smack your lips.
I know these mashed potatoes will be going to my hips,
And console myself with Malbec in reasonable sips.
> Winkler: I love that Heather put in the details of what the woman was eating and drinking

The ladies on my left are looking at their phones,
I hear the words "photographer" and "deejay,"
A mother and her daughter planning a big day,
I smile when they order your favorite soufflé.
Just one,
I know,
Doesn't sound like much fun,
Just one,
Only me,
In a world of twos,
Without you.

And finally, here's a song a student wrote to an image of jazz musicians in silhouette. Once again, he used the painting to set up a situation for him to write about, as if he was describing a movie. And he makes the larger point that in jazz all that matters is the music. You don't need to see the performers, have fancy choreography, or sets to enjoy the music.

"Jazz in Silhouette"
Lyrics by Mark Govatos (Used with Permission)

Verse #1
I was sitting in a jazz club on the Sunset Strip,
> Winkler: Nice specificity in setting up the location of the song

I came to hear a band they said could really rip.
They played Ellington's "A-Train" and "Blue Train" by Coltrane, I was thinking it was worth the trip.
> *This is where the writer shows his knowledge of jazz*

Then suddenly the lights went out all over the place,
> *Nice set up of the story*

You couldn't see a half a foot in front of your face,
Someone lit a candle behind the band's piano and you could just make out their shapes.

Chorus #1
The band was playing jazz in silhouette,
> *Finally, he reveals the painting*

No lights, no charts, no microphones, no sweat.
Those cats just closed their eyes and let their fingers do the rest,
The night the band played jazz in silhouette.

They never missed a fingering or fret.
If you think you've heard them play their best, you ain't seen nothin' yet.
'Til you hear the band play jazz in silhouette.

Bridge
I don't recall I ever saw the way those players looked,
> Nice philosophy of song in the bridge, and it's where you should put it

If they were young or old or in-between.
But I certainly remember the way that band could cook,
And the solos that made everybody scream.

13
GETTING OUTSIDE YOUR BUBBLE

When I was a young man, both my middle and high school had bands and choirs. Through them, I learned about the composers and artists that came before me, like John Philip Sousa, Stan Kenton, and Duke Ellington. I also remember being exposed to different classical composers like Aaron Copland, Leonard Bernstein, and Maurice Ravel in elementary school and in high school, my English teacher played current jazz artists Yusef Lateef and Ahmad Jamal in class and asked us to write stories about how the music made us feel.

Here's the stone-cold truth: as a songwriter, the more performers, lyricists, genres, and composers to which you are exposed will add to the different ways you can write and play a song. It's to your benefit to know what other people did before you. The great American popular song has been going for over a hundred years and there are a lot of valuable lessons you can pick up from the masters throughout all the decades.

Bruno Mars has made a large part of his career paying homage to other artists. Play his top ten hit from a few years ago, "Locked Out of Heaven" and then some songs by The Police and you'll hear that the grooves and production values are unmistakable. His song, "That's What I Like," which won the 2017 GRAMMY Song of the Year, borrows a lot from the new jack swing and R&B sound of the 1980s, when such stage lotharios as Johnny Gill and Bobby Brown would serenade the ladies in the audience. And of course, who can forget Bruno's 2014 smash, "Uptown Funk," which sounds a lot like a jam the Gap Band would do. It sounds so much like it, that the writers of the Gap Band sued Bruno and Mark Ronson and got their names added to the songwriting credits and will receive a share of the royalties.

Amy Winehouse, Adele, and Duffy all appropriated the style of soul singers like Etta James and Dinah Washington to craft their sounds. The list goes on and on—so why, as a nascent songwriter, should you miss out on this treasure trove? You'll broaden your songwriting style and maybe even win a GRAMMY to boot.

SONGWRITING ACTIONS

Below is a list of twenty performers and songwriters you should know. They are major innovators who have a lot to teach you. In my opinion, to know an artist, you must know three specific things about them. For example, if I asked you if you knew Elvis Presley, you could say, "The King of Rock 'n' Roll." Elvis is known for:

- "Hound Dog"
- Swiveling his hips
- Singing bluesy rhythm numbers
- Curling his lip
- The statement, "Elvis has left the building"
- Singing ballads in the style of crooners like Dean Martin
- Singing gospel music
- Recording for Sun Records

Here's the performers' list. Some of these artists (just a couple) are a little obscure, but they all have a lot to offer a songwriter in terms of different ways to write a song. However, at least thirteen or fourteen have had multiple hit songs that just about define their decade or genre of music:

1. Little Richard
2. Townes Van Zandt
3. Brian Wilson
4. Louis Jordan
5. Joni Mitchell

6. Louis Armstrong
7. Stephen Sondheim
8. Chuck Berry
9. Kurt Cobain
10. Lizzo
11. Loretta Lynn
12. TLC
13. The Andrews Sisters
14. Cole Porter
15. Bee Gees
16. David Bowie
17. Ed Sheeran
18. Antonio Carlos Jobim
19. Carole King
20. James Brown

How many did you know well enough that you have at least three things to list about them? For the ones you didn't know at all, pick out three, look them up, and read up on their lives and career achievements. Next, go to YouTube, look for videos of their songs that have views that are in the millions, and watch at least three or four. Then ask yourself the following questions:

1. What's their genre?
2. Did they have a predominating instrument in their music?
3. What were the rhythms of their tunes?
4. Did their songs have a limited or wide vocal range?
5. Were the lyrics simple or complicated?
6. What was the subject matter of their songs?
7. Did they have anything special that you never heard before? For instance, Little Richard's famous yell (which, by the way, Paul McCartney used in many of The Beatles' songs, such as "She Loves You").
8. What songwriting techniques did they use in their songs?

When you have researched three of the songwriter/performers you didn't know, choose one whose style is the most *unlike* yours. Then write a song in their style.

Winkler digresses:

About eight years ago, I had a very talented student named Angela Parrish. She had gone to music school in Kansas and upon graduation had come to Los Angeles in hopes of being a female jazz singer in the style of Diana Krall and Blossom Dearie. She played very good piano, had a wonderful voice, and wrote really cool songs. I gave her this assignment and she picked Townes Van Zandt, a very offbeat, underground, yet revered, songwriter from Texas and Nashville. After that assignment, she completely changed the direction of her career from jazz to Americana. So, you never know what this assignment will do to your songwriting trajectory. Angela went on to be one of the featured voices in the smash hit movie La La Land, *has two albums out, and a couple of movie soundtracks feature her songs. She's well worth checking out.*

Here are the attributes that come to my mind about the performers and songwriters on the list:

1. *Little Richard*: Pioneer of rock and roll, the fifties, played driving boogie-woogie piano, had a great scream, raw, up-tempo, flamboyant on stage, wore makeup and a huge pompadour, was outrageous
2. *Townes Van Zandt*: Nashville/Texas, outlaw, underground legend, played guitar, the seventies, wrote for Willie Nelson and Waylon Jennings, "Pancho and Lefty," his songs had simple forms, told stories
3. *Brian Wilson*: Pop superstar, leader of the Beach Boys, the sixties and seventies, incorporated harmonies and complex chords and melodies into pop music, wrote about surfing and cars, "Good Vibrations"—a masterpiece; played piano and guitar, great arranger, sang in a tenor range and falsetto
4. *Louis Jordan*: I love this guy! Merged forties boogie-woogie and race music* into fifties rock and roll, played sax, sang, up-tempo songs primarily, his songs were funny, clever lyrics, reminiscent of Cab Calloway, jazzy, walking bass was featured in his music
5. *Joni Mitchell*: Sixties to the eighties, queen of female singer/songwriters, played guitar with unusual tunings, "Both Sides Now," lived in Laurel Canyon, also played piano, wrote confessional lyrics about her love relationships, her songs were brilliant and verbose, delved into jazz

6. *Louis Armstrong*: Basically invented the jazz form, played trumpet and sang in a very gruff yet charming voice, "Hello Dolly," "What a Wonderful World," scat singer, a lot of up-tempo songs, the twenties to the sixties, great entertainer
7. *Stephen Sondheim*: Premiere Broadway musical theater composer from the late fifties to the two thousands, great lyricist, very intricate rhyming and clever wordplay, *West Side Story* lyrics, also wrote music, *Sweeney Todd* and *Into the Woods* can be very wordy, sophisticated
8. *Chuck Berry*: The fifties and sixties, called "The Father of Rock of Rock 'n' Roll" and is definitely one of its pioneers, a singer, songwriter, and guitarist, whose lyrics are heavily detailed descriptions of teen life, introduced guitar solos into rock music and his stage shows were theatrical and featured his "duck walking" across the stage, he was a major influence on subsequent rock acts such as Buddy Holly, the Beach Boys, and Prince
9. *Kurt Cobain*: Early nineties, cofounder, guitarist, lead singer, and primary songwriter of the Seattle-based group *Nirvana*, the voice of his generation, ushered in "grunge" music, an alternative form of rock music that was "rawer" and more angst-filled than the "corporate rock" music that was then popular
10. *Lizzo*: R&B and hip-hop influenced singer, songwriter, rapper, and flautist, her lyrics talk about accepting yourself for who you are physically, racially, and sexually, she is an advocate against body shaming, her stage persona is large, brassy, funny, and has roots in the soul music of the sixties and seventies
11. *Loretta Lynn*: Country queen of the sixties, "Coal Miner's Daughter," played guitar, wrote her own songs, dealt with many important topics of the sixties in songs, such as "The Pill," "Rated X," and "Dear Uncle Sam," had a more recent album produced by Jack White
12. *TLC*: Urban and hip-hop, female threesome, the nineties, "Waterfalls," "No Scrubs," rap and pop melodies, each member had identifiable character
13. *The Andrews Sisters*: Number one female harmony group of the forties, "Boogie Woogie Bugle Boy," "Rum and Coca-Cola," they really were sisters, made movies, associated with World War II-era, sang with Bing Crosby and the Mills Brothers, used jivey lyrics and big band rhythms

14. *Cole Porter*: Wrote both words and music, very sophisticated and urbane lyrics, sexually tinged, "Night and Day," "You're the Top," wrote a lot of laundry list songs, played piano, the twenties through the midsixties, wrote Broadway classics *Kiss Me Kate* and *Anything Goes*
15. *Bee Gees*: Group of three brothers, sang in falsetto and tight harmony, wrote their own songs, sounded "Beatle-ish" in early part of career, "To Love Somebody," "Words," embraced dance music with "Stayin' Alive," defined disco in the seventies, *Saturday Night Fever,* a lot of hits, the sixties through the eighties
16. *David Bowie*: The seventies and eighties, English singer/songwriter, one of the most influential musicians of the twentieth century, constantly changing and theatrical stage personalities (Ziggy Stardust and the Thin White Duke) were very influential in the music of the seventies and eighties, he could be pop "Modern Love," Rock "Rebel, Rebel," middle of the road "Little Drummer Boy," or avant-garde "Heroes"
17. *Ed Sheeran*: Melodic, guitar-oriented, folk, and pop meet rap-influenced verses, plays to loops, good classic lyric writing, tells stories, "Perfect," "The A Team," and "Shape of You," career started 2011, a lot of hits
18. *Antonio Carlos Jobim*: Father of "Bossa Nova"—a specific rhythm that comes from Brazil, the fifties through the nineties, played guitar, romantic, great melodies, sings without much vibrato, "The Girl from Ipanema," "Quiet Nights of Quiet Stars"
19. *Carole King*: Singer/songwriter, teenage Brill Building writer, hit songwriter, one of the most popular albums of all time, *Tapestry,* sixties to the two thousands, "(You Make Me Feel Like) A Natural Woman," "It's Too Late," "Will You Still Love Me Tomorrow?," R&B-influenced pop, plays piano
20. *James Brown*: Very rhythmic songs, all about the groove, great band, great dancer and performer, raspy rhythmic vocalist, "Papa's Got a Brand New Bag," proponent of Black pride, "Say It Loud—I'm Black and I'm Proud," the sixties to the eighties

GETTING OUTSIDE YOUR BUBBLE

Here's a song by my student Mark Govatos, inspired by learning more about the great Brazilian composer and lyricist Antonio Carlos Jobim:

"In the Middle of the Night"
Lyrics by Mark Govatos (Used with Permission)

When I close my eyes, I see you.
When your lips meet mine, I feel you.
Sometimes in the middle of the night.

When you wrap your arms around me,
I can feel your love surround me
> *Winkler: Nice picture, and "around me" and "surround me" are double rhymes*

Sometimes in the middle of the night.

Crimson skies at sunset, but any time's the right time
> *Nice specific imagery and it's alliterative*

For kissing as we stroll along the beach.
> *Involves the beach that a lot of bossa nova songs have as a location*

A fateful love like ours could last a thousand lifetimes,
> *Hyper romantic*

Or at least until the morning comes and shakes me from this dream.

My students Molly Cotton and Lilianna Wilde wrote this song in the style of Louis Jordan. It really captures his fun and humorous take on lyrics:

"He's Not Much to Look at (But He's Mine, All Mine)"
Lyrics by Molly Cotton and Lilianna Wilde (Used with Permission)

He's losing all his hair,
Holes in his underwear,
> *Winkler: Great specifics in the A section*

He ain't so debonair,
He's not much to look at but he's mine, all mine.

His lips aren't much to kiss,
No sugar on his grits,
Toes to his fingertips,
> *Great line—so much personality*

He's not much to look at, but he's mine, all mine.

Last Sunday he came over for dinner,
> *I love it when the bridge is a complete scene that you can see*

Got down on one knee with a ring,
I never saw a rock that was bigger:
Woo baby! Wouldn't change a thing.
> *Great conversational stinger and payoff line*

14
WRITING TO AN EXISTING MELODY

What comes first? The words or the music? Whenever I tell people I'm a lyricist, that's usually the first question they ask. And my answer to them is, "It depends." Sometimes I write the lyric first and give it to the melody writer, and sometimes I get the melody and write the lyrics to it. Actually, I like to mix it up.

And writing lyrics to a finished melody is a great way to meet some wonderful musicians. It's not a skill every lyricist has. I can't tell you the number of times I've turned in a lyric, and the writer told me, "You didn't change my melody! Thanks so much!!" By being able to write a lyric to a finished melody, I have written with writers such as Dean Gant (who's written for artists Anita Baker and Peabo Bryson) and with David Pomeranz (Barry Manilow, Bette Midler, and Kenny Rogers). And as a lyricist, I have written songs with K-pop writers, country writers, rockers, sensitive singer/songwriter types, and cabaret and Broadway musical tunesmiths.

And of course, I've met many A-list jazz composers/performers in the business by writing lyrics to their existing jazz melodies. I've actually made lifelong songwriting partners and met people I never would have met any other way.

Winkler digresses . . .

I recorded my first jazz album, Jazz Life, *in 1981. It was released in 1982 on a small label outside of Seattle, called First American. The album was very much in the style of Michael Franks, Al Jarreau, and The Manhattan Transfer. It's plainly a jazz record—but with plenty of pop touches—and I wrote the songs with the same techniques I first learned in Al Kasha's class and that I've honed through the years. Surprisingly,* Jazz Life *did quite well on jazz radio stations. But the dirty little secret about my first record is that I recorded it with the musicians with whom I'd been doing all my pop demos. So, when I decided to make my second record, I drew up a list of jazz greats that I'd like to work with: David Benoit, Joe Sample, Robert Kraft, and Dave Grusin.*

Over the next few years, I wound up writing with three of the four—including Joe Sample. When I was a young man, I loved Joe's piano playing, first with the Jazz Crusaders and then on his solo albums. In particular, there was one tune I played over and over, "Night Flight," from his album, The Hunter. *It was even in my key! I wrote lyrics for the song, and then did a good demo of it, with me singing over the track. Through a friend I managed to get the demo to Joe Sample's manager.*

About a month later, at about 9:00 p.m. one night, I got a call from Joe Sample telling me he really liked my lyric, but he'd like to meet with me in the upcoming week to work on a couple of lyric changes he had in mind. At the time, Joe Sample was a big star, so I was more than happy to meet with him. When the song was done, I asked him if he would play on my album, and he said yes.

How did I get Joe Sample to do this? I wasn't on a label at the time, and though Jazz Life *had done pretty well in the jazz world, I was far from a known entity. The only reason I can come up with is that my lyric was good. Over the years, I've worked with many jazz musicians, and they get many amateur lyrics sent to them for their jazz tunes, and about 90 percent are terrible. Never underestimate the power of excellence in the world of music— it's opened many doors for me, and it can do the same for you.*

One funny aside. On the day before the session, I got a call from Joe's manager asking me to what studio should they deliver Joe's nine-foot grand piano. Well, at the time, my album was self-financed, and I couldn't spring for the $500 cost of the piano delivery. Luckily, Joe said he'd play on the

WRITING TO AN EXISTING MELODY

studio piano. It turns out that it's the same piano Bruce Hornsby played on for his massive hit record, "The Way It Is."

More digressions . . .

A couple of years ago, Claire Martin phoned me and asked me to write some lyrics for a tribute album she was going to be recording, featuring the songs of Wes Montgomery. Claire is a world-class singer, who over the years has done quite a few of my songs and has become a good friend. I love Wes Montgomery too. When I was in high school, I was taken by his unique style of playing and the incredible albums he made with Creed Taylor. Claire asked me to write lyrics for Wes's tune called "Bumpin" and I said, "That's my favorite song of his!" Soon thereafter, I wrote a lyric with my wonderful lyric cowriter, Shelley Nyman, and we called the new song, "I Could Get Used to This."

When I played it for Claire, she flipped for it and then asked me to write a couple more songs from the Wes Montgomery songbook. Which I did. Then, about a week later—in the middle of the night—I woke up with one question on my mind. Did Claire have the publisher's permission to do this? Of course, she did, I thought, and went back to sleep.

As you now know, I've put lyrics to jazz songs many times in the past and *the rule is to get in contact with the publisher first* and see if they are open to having a lyric written to their song. Some are and some aren't. Sometimes, the catalogues of these jazz greats are run by warring families or by very protective publishers or large corporations that can't be bothered. You must reach out and see what the story is. The lyric you write can be sensational, but sometimes there can be extenuating circumstances you know nothing about. Here's my lyric for the Wes Montgomery jazz classic, "Bumpin'":

"I Could Get Used to This"
Music by John L. Montgomery
Lyrics by Mark Winkler and Shelley Nyman

I could get used to this,
    Winkler: Always the title goes in the first or last line of the A section
Feelin' fine.

> *This is a laundry list song; I'm listing the nice things I can get used to*
Talkin' all through the night,
No sense of time.

I could get used to this,
Words that you said;
Champagne in coffee cups,
> *Great furniture and it's alliterative*
Breakfast in bed.

I could get used to this,
Not bein' blue.
But why haven't I told you,
> *This sets up my problem quite nicely*
When I know that it's true.

I called Claire, and, unfortunately, she had collected about eight different lyrics from three different lyricists including me, but hadn't called Wes Montgomery's publisher. Somehow, I was chosen to make the call. I must admit, while professional, the woman on the other end of the line was fairly intimidating. I told her that I had written lyrics for "Bumpin," one of Wes's most famous instrumentals and she quickly informed me that over the last forty years many lyricists had tried their hand with the song, but she had not granted them the rights. My heart sank! I asked her if I could send her a demo of my lyric and she agreed. Amazingly, she called me back quickly (in showbiz, if you get a call back quickly, it's almost always good news) and told me she loved my lyric and would grant the publishing rights to me as the lyricist, along with Shelley.

Now I was cocky, so I submitted my other Wes Montgomery lyrics and she promptly rejected them! In my humble opinion, the lyrics were great, but it is the publisher's prerogative to grant permission. So, scope out the situation first.

From the thirties to the sixties, it was common for lyricists to take melodies that had been hits in other countries and put English lyrics to them. Wordsmiths like Johnny Mercer ("Autumn Leaves") and Sammy Cahn ("Bei

Mir Bist Du Schoen") wrote many songs this way. Here's just a small list of standards that started out as songs in another language:

- "Despacito"—Spanish
- "Beyond the Sea"—French
- "Mack the Knife"—German
- "What a Diff'rence a Day Makes"—Spanish
- "What Now My Love?"—French
- "Volaré"—Italian
- "99 Luftballoons"—German
- "It's Impossible"—Spanish
- "Life Goes On"—Korean
- "My Way"—French

Unfortunately, this practice has fallen out of favor. Just a couple of songs over the last few decades have been translated into English such as "The Macarena" and "Gloria." And remember, all of ABBA's greatest hits were first written in Swedish. But even though this practice is not popular, that doesn't mean you shouldn't do it. I think it's an ideal situation for the lyricist.

Here are all the pluses to doing it: if the song has been a hit in another country, you already know that the melody works and the general feel of the song is a winner. So, for you as a lyricist, you have the luxury of writing to a great melody and track. If the publisher likes the song and grants you a license for the English lyrics, you have forged a good connection with a publisher and probably even the hit writer or group that wrote the original song. No downside as far as I can see.

So, how do you go about writing lyrics to an instrumental or foreign-language song?

- First, get a track and sheet music for the song. Then, listen to the song while reviewing the sheet music until you memorize it.
- Now identify the form, which will tell you where to put the title. If the form is AABA, the title is the first or last line of the first A section.
  - If the form is verse/chorus, the title is generally in the first line, last line, or every line of the chorus.

- When you figure out where the title goes, you have to literally count the number of syllables in the title. For instance, if it's five syllables, go to your title folder and look for any titles that are five syllables. I can't tell you how many times a title from my title folder with the appropriate number of syllables has worked. It's uncanny.
- Once you have the title, come up with the story plot that fits the title and then write the lyrics, knowing what you must accomplish in each section of the tune. I like to know what the general story of the song is in the original language, it can sometimes be wonderful, and inform your lyric, but I'm not a slave to it. The important thing is creating a lyric that compliments the melody and is interesting and believable.
- Often, a title or a line of lyric will suggest itself. The melody gives you so much. As I always say—a great melody is worth about 70 percent of the song.
- Write exactly to the notes you are given—don't approximate. You can't legally change a composer's melody. Plus, a good composer knows where every note of their melody should be and doesn't want you coming along approximating their melody. I've had composers practically cry because I didn't change a note of their melody. If the composer has a good voice have them sing it. If they don't, have them play the notes on a guitar or piano.
- I also ask the composer if they have a title for the song, or if they have a story that that inspired the song. I remember asking a wonderful pianist and composer friend of mine, Louis Durra, what he called a particular instrumental of his that I liked, and he said, "How to Pack a Suitcase." With a title like that, the song practically wrote itself.
- Many times, the composer will tell you invaluable info about the song that will make your job easier. My job as a lyricist is done if I get the title and a really great concept. Sometimes I get it from the composer.

SONGWRITING ACTIONS

Write English lyrics to a foreign song or instrumental. Since this is an exercise, don't worry about getting the publisher's permission.

Here are some foreign songs and instrumentals you can try:

- Karol G and Shakira's "TQC"

- Manuel Turizo's "La Bachata"
- Louanne's "Secret"
- Maluma and Marc Anthony's "La Formula"
- Billy Childs's "The End of Innocence"
- David Benoit's "Dad's Room"
- Balbina's "Das Kaputtgehen"
- Alan Pasqua's "Ellingtonia"

Or pick a foreign language hit and write English lyrics to it. To find foreign hits, just Google the top hits of a particular country. For example: "Top Hits of France 2024" or "Top Hits of Mexico 2024."

Remember,

- Figure out the form, it will tell you where to place the title.
- Play the song over and over until you learn the melody.
- Come up with the title and place it in the right section of the form.
- Come up with a story concept based on the title.
- Write the lyrics.

15
PERFORMING LIVE

Like me, a lot of songwriters in my classes are also performers. I've been touring and singing at different clubs and festivals all over the world for more than thirty years. I was not born a great performer, but through the years I've learned some hard-earned lessons about performing and being on the road. Once I got the hang of it, performing to a live audience is one of the most satisfying things I do. And in todays' world, now that streaming and digital downloads have reduced revenues for songwriters and artists, live performance is where the money is.

Mark with Cheryl Bentyne singing live at the Los Angeles County Museum of Art Friday Night Jazz Series (photo by Craig Levine, used by permission).

Here's what I learned the hard way:

1. *Only do a maximum of three new songs per show.* You do not need to do a whole new selection of songs every time you perform. Doing songs that you've already done leaves more time in rehearsal for the new songs. Then, if you follow my rule number 2, it gives you the security of knowing that no matter how well the new tunes go over, you have some "road-tested" songs that work. Once I have a solid beginning and closing for my show, I tend to keep them for many years. That's how important they are. Willie Nelson has been singing "Whiskey River" for over forty years as his opener. You need an opening song that you really have under your belt. In addition to saving you time in rehearsal, you have one more tune in your set you can knock out of the park because the minute you hit the stage there are millions of other things that suddenly come to mind, like:

   "Oh no, I can't hear myself!"
   "Wow, this is a full house, and the crowd is really receptive!" or "Where is everybody?"
   "The stage has a sprung floor and I'm bouncing up here."
   "There's my old friend and his new wife in the front row, I haven't seen him for years."

   It hits you at once and you want a song that you could continue singing even if a bomb went off next to you. You want your closing song to be an emotional and musical peak of the show. The kind of song that incites the audience to want to bring you back for an encore.

2. *Record your performance.* Video's best (but audio works as well). It shows you what you do right, and it shows you what you did wrong. It can break you of some bad vocal and physical habits (e.g., making faces or smiling during a sad song). Performers who say they can't record their shows because they don't like the way they look or sound need to get over it. At first, we all are surprised at the reality of our performance. But the more you see yourself, the more reality takes over.

   Most importantly, it tells you to which songs the audience responds, and which ones aren't grabbing them. If you have at least a quarter of a house, the response should be fairly reliable from show to show in telling you what songs are reaching the audience. And remember, no matter how much you like a song that you wrote, the audience is never wrong. I literally count how long their applause lasts. Plus, if there are whoops and cheers after a song, even better. If, after a song, there is little applause ("crickets") and people are coughing and talking during the song, these are all bad signs. The only thing I notice is that, generally, ballads get less applause than my more "energetic" songs. However, after the show featuring some of my best ballads, people come up to me to tell me how much they liked the slow song that made them cry. The songs that the audience likes will become your "tentpole" tunes that your set will be built around.

Winkler digresses . . .
I was doing an album-release concert for my album, Till I Get It Right, *and about two weeks before the gig I wrote a funny song with my piano accompanist, Jamieson Trotter, called "Somewhere in Brazil (In the Valley)" that wasn't on the album. However, it was a really cute number and I decided to put it in the show at the last minute. What do you know? The new song was the smash of the night; the audience roared. Afterward, people asked me if the new song was on my new album—which of course, it wasn't. Lesson learned: when you're doing a show to promote a new album, don't perform a song that's not on it.*

3. *Know your tentpole tunes.* These are the songs you knock out of the park. You can identify them because they're the ones that get the most applause and enthusiastic comments after a show. Keep them in your set and weave your new material around these songs. Even if a new song gets tepid applause, you've got the tentpole song coming up next to keep the momentum of the show going. Surprisingly, tentpole tunes work in almost every venue and in front of every crowd. They are worth their weight in gold.
4. *The sound person is your friend.* Make sure you can hear yourself in the monitors. I like to have two monitors in front of me, placed like ears at each side. Don't have too much reverb on the sound; it can mess with

your pitch. Go out of your way to have a good relationship with the sound person. Ask their name as soon as you arrive and be sure to remember it.

5. *Dress like you're appearing at the most prestigious venue of your genre.* Look like you'd like to be seen in a perfect world. Don't dress like you just came from work. Look at the successful performers who are most like you and style yourself accordingly.
6. *Have "musician-proof" charts.* Most solo acts don't travel with a band, or even a keyboard player. Make sure your music is easy to read, legible, and has clear notation for everything that makes the arrangement special to you. I used to have the worst charts, with a lot of confusing changes and handwritten edits on them. Don't waste valuable rehearsal time spending ten minutes explaining what you want during a two-and-a-half hour rehearsal of ten or twelve tunes. Always start a rehearsal with a couple of easy tunes to get your chops warmed up and to get everyone's spirits high, then give them the bad boy that may be a little more challenging to play.
7. *Don't speak to musicians in "singer-ese."* It's not that difficult to learn the standard language of your craft: take a class in music theory. Sit down with a friendly musician and go through your charts to make sure you know the correct terms for all the components of your song. The more you can speak to musicians in their language, the better it will be for you.
8. *Sing songs that flatter your voice.* Choose material that shows off your "money notes" or highlights the best things you do vocally. Once again, recording yourself helps. You know your best notes, the best keys for your arrangements, and your comfortable range; check them at the piano or with your guitar.
9. *Tell your own story with your songs.* Each song should come authentically from you. It should reflect how you feel and where you've been. Don't sing a song if it means nothing to you emotionally. People love performers because they love their stories, and who they are, probably more than they like their voices and their songs. Each song should let the audience know more about you.
10. *Have interesting arrangements of your tunes.* If you're singing a song from the Great American Songbook, Ella or Frank have probably done it about as good as it can be done. If you're singing a current hit, you're not going to beat Bruno Mars or Ariana Grande. You have to either pick less

well-known songs (which I highly recommend) or find a way into well-known songs that is different. But true to yourself—a great arrangement can do that. Recently, I watched a documentary on Tina Turner and one of the highlights was her reworking of The Beatles' "Help." The original was up-tempo, but Tina slowed it down and made it a very personal statement about her life that really resonated with the audience.

11. *Know what you're going to say.* Don't go on stage without an idea of what you're going to say to introduce yourself and your songs to the audience. Magic will not happen. You won't suddenly be brilliant and screamingly funny. You've got to plan it. Set up the song. Talk about why you're singing it, a bit of background on the song, and who you are. Performers from Bruce Springsteen to Barbra Streisand are masters at putting the songs they sing in context. I always write what I'm going to say and rehearse in the mirror until I'm comfortable with it. When in doubt, don't talk at all; bad stage patter can literally ruin a live show.

12. *Be in your comfort zone.* Whatever you do onstage is going to be better if you do it while relaxed, in the moment, and in command of your material. Never do anything onstage that is so challenging or out of your range that it robs your whole set of you being present. I think it is always better to do a song you're comfortable with than one you're worried about. Having that one challenging song you don't quite have under your belt can take focus away from the whole show. In the early part of my career, that one difficult song ruined many a set.

13. *Singing live is all about energy.* Recording is about technical perfection and nailing the take that has just the right emotion. However, performing live is more about energy—the kind you bring to the audience and the kind the audience gives to you. I recommend only one or two ballads in a twelve- or thirteen-song set. There's a saying in show business: "You've got to earn your ballads," which means a live show needs to have *momentum* to work. Too many ballads get in the way of that and make it harder to keep the audience with you. A variety of rhythms, tempos, and keys is your friend when you perform live. There are some singers who kill it live because they literally hit the stage like a blowtorch, but who aren't as good in a studio, when suddenly the technical aspects of singing are put in the spotlight. Singing live is not about perfection but about connection with the audience, giving them entertainment and a good show. They're

Mark singing live with his trio at KSDS in San Diego (photo by Larry Redman, used by permission).

already on your side—they've carved out their evening for you and spent money for the tickets, they want to like you. Learn how to harness your energy.

14. *Rest on the road.* When I'm traveling and touring, I make sure I get enough rest. You want your energy to peak during the show. If possible, don't arrive at the venue straight from a plane; rehearse for two hours and then do a gig. Don't party all night and blow your voice out after the show. Remember, there'll be another one tomorrow. Being a singer can be tough. Vocal cords are delicate things that get affected rather quickly by stress, fatigue, and overuse. Take care of your instrument—it's the only one you've got. Sometimes I feel like a party pooper—I get that when you're in a new city you want to explore it, but your priorities have to be the show first, last, and always.

A few years ago, a friend asked me to write about the worst gig I ever had, and I thought it would be fun to let you in on a particularly stressful moment in my performing life, which now many years later only seems funny.

My Gig from Hell . . .

It was 1987. Reagan was president. I dressed like Don Johnson in "Miami Vice" and my album Ebony Rain was getting a lot of airplay in Los Angeles.

I received a call from this lovely club in Santa Monica, At My Place (sadly no longer there), to open for a really hot group on MCA, the Perri Sisters. They were sensational—and I was excited to be part of it all.

The day of the gig, we did the soundcheck at the club. The drummer was playing exceedingly loud and the saxophonist was heavily into his David Sanborn thing, but the pianist was cool.

My bass player at the time, while incredibly likeable and a great player, had an eye for the ladies. My backup singer Beth was already standing on the opposite side of the stage from him to avoid his endless pickup lines, but I must admit that when he started "poppin'" he was great. "Poppin'" was a surefire thing that bass players did in the eighties (think Earth Wind & Fire) to drive the audiences (and yes, the ladies) wild and this dude was the king!

As we were doing the soundcheck, the waitresses were setting up and Matt Kramer, the manager of the club, was pacing around. He was all business and somewhat brusque, but he knew his stuff and I definitely wanted to be playing his club again, so I tried to do the soundcheck in my allotted time.

Now, it's five minutes until showtime and no bass player. Then it's five minutes past showtime and no bass player. Matt Kramer, with his no-bullshit manner, comes up to me and says, "Hey man, you're on," and I say, "There's no way I can be on, my bass player is missing and the only thing I can do now is a ballad, and I that's not a good way to start a set."

The next thing I knew, I was on stage with my band playing this lovely ballad. However, it's Saturday night, the drinks have been imbibed, and the ballad is not cutting it. In the still silence of a "get off the stage" vibe, Matt comes up to the lip of the stage and hands me a cocktail napkin with this message written on it:

"Man, I'm sorry, I've been in a freeway accident. I'll be there for the second set. Your bass player."

There are the moments that define a performer's life. This was one of them. I could have walked off the stage and cleared it for the act for which the audience was breathlessly waiting. I could have committed professional suicide by doing a whole set of ballads, but to be honest with you, I found the cocktail napkin message so outrageous that I shared it with the audience. Guess what, they found it hilarious.

Right after I got this big laugh, the fantastic bass player of the Perri Sisters, John Baker, yelled from the back of the house, "I'll play bass for you!" From that minute on, I was home free. Every number was a three-act play: John was presented with the chart, he furrowed his brow while I asked him, "Can you do it?" and after a dramatic pause, he would nod his head "yes" and then knock it out of the park. He's a great bass player and my charts weren't that hard, but to the audience every note executed was a marvel.

After the show, I was showered with praise, the manager came up to me and wanted me back, and then a waitress motioned to talk to me—in private. She looked exhausted and pissed. As I said, it was a full house—but the reason she was so upset was that she had worked twice as many tables as usual during the first set: hers and those of the waitress my bass player had been "poppin'" back at his apartment. She filled in all the details—and I still have the cocktail napkin.

SONGWRITING ACTIONS

These actions are primarily for the songwriter/performers reading this book. I have found that a large percentage of my songwriting students are also performers.

1. Record your next performance. You can record it with your voice memo or video app on your phone. This only works if you are performing in a room that's at least a quarter filled.
2. A few days after your performance, listen to the applause at the end of each song and count the number of beats they get. The average is around twenty-three beats. If there are whoops and hollers, all the better.
3. Notice which songs get crickets (silence) or less applause. If there's a lot of talking or coughing, that's a negative.
4. Write down the two or three songs in your set that get the most applause and use them as the pegs to build your show around next time. Put the numbers you aren't sure about in-between them.
5. If you're watching video of yourself, notice if you have any annoying habits or physical tics. I've mentioned my crazy right arm that keeps going up

on me during a song (I'm working on it). Having your eyes closed, making faces, and walking around too much are also habits to be avoided on stage.
6. Pay attention to your patter and notice if you are talking too much, that your patter doesn't set up the song properly, or is nonsensical. Generally, shorter is better.
7. You can also notice if you're singing on pitch, if you're supporting your voice properly, and if the group is supporting you or overpowering you.

OBJECTIVES OF THE SONGWRITING ACTIONS
- To find out which songs of yours are scoring with your audience
- To find out if you have any annoying physical habits while singing
- To find out if you are singing properly and that your stage patter is to the point and sets up the songs properly

And to think, all this knowledge comes from the simple act of recording your performance for free on your phone. If you have a hard time doing this at first, ask one of your "gatekeepers" to help you. Remember, a gatekeeper is someone who has a little bit more knowledge than you at this point but has no hidden agendas. They are there to support you—but also to tell you if you're doing something wrong.

16
BREAK TIME!

A lot of assignments! A lot of songs! You're tired, so take a break with the answers to two questions that I get a lot.

As a teacher, one frequently asked question I get is, "What do I do when I'm stuck?"

It happens to all of us who write songs. We're riding along on inspiration (or maybe just a really good cup of java), feelin' like we can do anything, when suddenly we reach the second verse or the bridge and oops!! The little engine that could—can't—we're stuck. Our excitable and imaginative child is suddenly replaced by our ever-lurking and critical adult (usually your mother) telling you, "You aren't that great," "The song is nothing," and worse yet, in your head you're thinking . . .

SO, HOW DO I FINISH THIS SONG?

Here are some tried and true tips I've used over the years to get over the bump—and I hope they work for you.

In no particular order:

1. It's always the basics. I find that nine times out of ten, it's the elemental stuff you know like the back of your hand that trips you up. For instance, you're not writing to title, you aren't telling the whole story, you're leaving details out. And, heaven forbid, you aren't fulfilling what each section of

the song must accomplish. And just like a car that can run for quite a while without servicing, you suddenly stop.
2. Is your story/concept clear? This happens to me a lot. I get a great title and rush into writing the song, and I don't do a really clear two-sentence description of what the title is about. In that case, I will go to a patient friend and tell them the story of my song. I always find there are things in the telling that I can use to sharpen my story.
3. You put too much story or details into the first verse. This happens frequently to budding songwriters—they put too much in the first verse and don't have anything to say in the others. So, carve out some story, use the space to put in details like how the singer is feeling or make sure you've answered—*who, what, when,* and *where*.
4. Just write anything in the section of the tune you are stuck on. It doesn't have to be good, just fill in the words and move on. Short-circuit your inner critic. Writing a bad song isn't like killing someone—society will forgive you. (I forgave will.i.am a long time ago for writing "My Humps.") Then, when you come back to the song in an hour or two or the next day, you can change the bad lines that bugged you. Songwriting is a process, and the song will reveal itself to you over time. When I write a song, I can think it's wonderful—terrible—needs improvement—then wonderful, all in the same sitting. Only time and playing it for a few people will determine its real worth. Just finish it.
5. What did you leave out? Then put that in the song.
6. Take a break from the song and walk the dog or take a shower. I often go to sleep thinking about the song I'm writing. In the morning, I usually can solve quite a few of the problems I was wrestling with the night before.
7. Bring in a cowriter who can help you out of your jam. I love to work with cowriters and bounce ideas off them. Different people have different viewpoints and different ways of looking at the same situation. They have different skills that can complement your skills. However, never work with anyone who is not at your level. They'll take you down faster than you can lift them up.
8. Drink another cup of coffee, go to the beach, play a great song you wish you had written, read a good review you've received.
9. If none of these things work and the song doesn't get any better, dump it and start over. Every time I've done this, the second song is always better.

That's because all of the things I've done to make the first song work have prepared me for the second song.

Here's another question I'm asked a lot . . .

SO, HOW DO I KNOW IF MY SONG IS ANY GOOD?

As artists, we have to face a painful reality—we all live in bubbles. I think internet algorithms have had a lot to do with it. They learn your tastes and then feed us what they think we want to see and experience, leaving out other ideas and topics that might challenge us and educate us in other ways.

Facebook and Instagram are probably the worst offenders. Most likely, we all have seven friends on Facebook who love whatever we say or pictures we post. I know who mine are; I love them, who wouldn't? They unequivocally love me, but I don't get my sense of reality from them.

I've seen too many of my friends post ugly pictures of themselves and then see their seven friends post "handsome" and "looking good." Or my songwriting students post fuzzy live videos of their mediocre songs—where they look bad and sound worse—and guess what? The seven friends write, "Love the song" and "You sound great."

So, what do you do? You have to get "gatekeepers" to keep you honest. Not your friends and definitely not your family (they'll either love everything you do or hate everything you do), but professionals in the fields you want to go into (teachers, producers, and critics) or really talented artists who are a couple of rungs up the ladder from you. Get their opinions about your work—your singing and songs. Pick their brains and then take a deep breath and take notes.

How do you find these qualified "critics"? You network, you go to clubs and see who the good performers are, or you take classes and figure out who are the stars in the room, or you go to teachers and critics in your field. And you take them out to lunch and ask them questions. (Most experts can be had for lunch!)

Send them no more than three of your songs and then (gasp) ask them which ones they liked, what was their favorite, and was there anything you could improve on? And then be prepared for a little "reality." I should put in a disclaimer here, I don't think you should listen to everything people say and view it as the gospel truth no matter how learned or skilled the person is, but if the same type of comment keeps coming up three, four, or more times, I'd definitely think about it. I let what these "gatekeepers" say wash over me—which means I don't challenge or process them at the time they come in. I let the comments brew in my mind, and the criticisms that are valid linger in my mind. But if two or three of these unbiased experts like your tunes, the song is good. Now, I believe a good song can take you quite far in this business—and a great one even further. But there are a lot of other factors involved in show business, like how you present yourself, business acumen, and plain luck and timing. It's always amazing the things you learn when you open yourself up to an expert opinion.

Winkler digresses . . .

Which brings me to my moment of truth. I was producing a new CD and working with a very talented piano player, arranger, and conductor. We had some things in common—we both loved jazz and singers (especially the one we were working with) and were from California. But we had a lot of differences: I was a lot older than he; I wasn't as crazy about long instrumental solos as he was, and I generally liked simpler arrangements. At first, it drove me crazy to be collaborating with him; we had some fiery moments. But after each "discussion," I was impressed with his passion and smarts. There is always more than one way to approach anything. And to be honest with you, I'm a little spoiled. I work with some of the most talented people in the world who share a lot of my views on music. It all goes down very easily with a lot of camaraderie and smiles. However, this guy didn't fit the mold.

But somewhere near the end of the project, when I was mixing the tracks, the mixes weren't coming together as I would have liked. I played them for him, and guess what: this kid came in and by hearing things differently than me, saved it! The mixes suddenly sounded great. He had different tools in his tool belt and some of them were just what was needed.

I want to thank him for having his own ears, it expanded my horizons—and I've grown. He wasn't one of my seven friends on Facebook and I'm all the better for it.

17

WRITING FOR THE MUSICAL THEATER

I've always loved musicals. My Aunt Shirley, a fellow musical junkie, would always have the latest Broadway show albums in a special wire LP holder next to her turntable. As a teenager in the 1960s, the first thing I'd do when I hit her apartment was to look for what new treats she had to offer. She had the hits like *West Side Story* and *The Sound of Music*, but she also had little-known gems like *Subways Are for Sleeping* and *The Apple Tree*.

I was tuned into Broadway deep cuts even then, and I remember I would ask her to play me "A Quiet Thing" from *Flora the Red Menace* written by Kander and Ebb and sung by Judy Garland's young daughter Liza Minnelli. I'd ask to hear Molly Picon sing something by the then up-and-comer Jerry Herman, who had just written his first show, *Milk and Honey*. And we always played Barbra Streisand. As far as we were concerned, we discovered her. My Aunt Shirley even had her recording of "Miss Marmelstein" from *I Can Get It for You Wholesale*, a much less-successful musical that came out a few years before her star-making role in *Funny Girl*. Living in California, I didn't go to that many musicals, but I did see the hit shows from Broadway showcased on TV, as well as some touring companies when they played L.A. and, of course, I watched the movie versions of the big Broadway shows.

At the start of my career, I thought I'd like to try my hand at writing lyrics for a Broadway show. I didn't go in that direction until the midnineties when my husband's best friend, Bob Schrock, became the artistic director of the

Celebration Theatre in Los Angeles. This small, respected company specializes in works representing the LGBTQ+ experience. He had success with a show called *The Gay '90s Musical: Looking Back . . . Moving On*, which was basically a musical revue about being gay in that decade. It was a really cute show and I remember sitting in the theater after the performance wondering why he hadn't asked me to write a song for it! But that was soon remedied when Bob approached me to write for another musical revue he had in mind, titled *Naked Boys Singing!* I've already talked about the success of that show, so I won't say too much more about it, except that it was a big hit in L.A. and then in New York, and suddenly I was knee-deep in musical theater.

The sixty-five-seat Celebration Theatre, where *Naked Boys Singing!* started, was just five minutes down the hill from my house. I was there most nights watching the show, drinking in its success, and selling a lot of CDs that I had produced on my own label, Café Pacific Records (a theatrical producer/boutique musical theater label had been set to produce it, when, surprisingly, they pulled out before the great reviews and acclaim had started happening. I always used to torture the producer who turned us down by reminding him of how many CDs I had sold of our little show). We never produced a specific cast recording for the New York production, but hawked the L.A. album with an updated cover showing the New York artwork and cast and sold even more copies.

Winkler digresses . . .

I produced the original cast recording of Naked Boys Singing! *with two dynamos: the show's director Bob Schrock and its musical director, Stephen Bates. One of the lucky breaks we had with* NBS! *was that the original L.A. cast was exceptionally talented. So, here we are working on the original cast recording, in a lovely home studio with a sympathetic engineer, Tom Griep, flush from all the success we were having with great reviews and sold-out audiences, but something wasn't going right. The big group opening number, "Gratuitous Nudity," was the first song we recorded, and it felt lifeless and strangely joyless. What could be wrong? After much discussion, we realized that these young men were doing seven shows a week totally naked. To them, belting out the songs and being naked were the way they felt most comfortable. So, voilá!, soon clothes were shed, and the song sounded great! After all, it wasn't called* Naked Boys Singing! *for nothing.*

Over the last twenty years, I've written six musicals (one has been a smash and two of them have played all over the country to great audiences and reviews). Through these shows, I've learned a lot about the dos and don'ts while writing for the theater. Therefore, I present . . .

TOP TIPS FOR WRITING THEATER SONGS

It's always about "The Book": I tell my students that when it comes to writing a musical, it's all about the libretto (the story-driven script), called a "book" in musical theater parlance. So, the initial step is to come up with the plot and dialogue first. If you're not that kind of writer, work with someone who is or option the rights to someone else's great novel or story outline—no ifs, ands, or buts. Ever since *Showboat* (based on Edna Ferber's best-selling 1926 novel of the same name) and *Oklahoma!* (based on Lynn Riggs's 1930 stage play, *Green Grow the Lilacs*), the musical is driven by a story and is not just a pastiche of songs with a silly plot to waste your time until the next big production number comes along.

All the rules apply: Just because your songs are now going to be in a musical doesn't mean they don't have to follow the same rules of good songwriting as before. I can't tell you how many times I've heard poorly written songs in musicals. It's almost as though the dramatic structure of a musical has given these newbie writers permission to be self-indulgent and unfocused.

The song must further the action: As opposed to a typical pop song, a song in a show must move the story along. The character or characters must have a realization, and/or perhaps a resolution of conflict. What's most important is that they emerge at a different place from where they started the song.

Song craft is paramount: This is the genre that values classic songwriting techniques more than any other. Perfect rhymes, three rhymes, alliteration, and clarity are prized in writing for the theater. Intelligence and a certain sophistication are of paramount importance.

The lyric must reflect each character's voice: Much like dialogue in a musical, the song must reflect the voice of the character singing it. In *Wicked*, Glinda's lyrics are full of Southern California "Valley Girl" colloquialisms. In George Gershwin's *Porgy and Bess* (technically, an opera), the lyrics reflect the voices of 1920s African American residents of Charleston, South Carolina's, "Catfish Row" neighborhood.

You always wind up killing your favorite child: This is a very dramatic way of saying (and believe me, making musical theater is all about drama) that somehow when writing a show, you wind up having to cut your favorite song before the show opens. I've seen this happen in almost every show I've written. Moving the story along is of prime importance, and sometimes that killer song you love with all your heart just lies there. While you're admiring its craft, and that clever rhyme you've come up with in the second verse, the audience is waiting for the next plot point to happen.

HERE ARE SOME DIFFERENT TYPES OF THEATER SONGS

The "I want" song: This is generally sung by the protagonist of the musical at the beginning of the show. It details the character's motives and agenda. Think of *My Fair Lady*'s Eliza Doolittle singing "Wouldn't It be Loverly?" or when the *Beauty and the Beast*'s Belle sings "Belle," or "I Want to be a Producer" in *The Producers*.

The "charm" song: This is a song that makes you smile and endears the character to the audience. It literally charms them out of their seats. Think the young Fanny Brice singing, "I'm the Greatest Star" from *Funny Girl* or Edna and her husband's song-and-dance number, "Timeless to Me" in *Hairspray*.

The comedy song: This is an out-and-out funny song with a lot of big laughs such as "Big Ass Rock" from *The Full Monty*, "I'm Just a Girl Who Cain't Say No" from *Oklahoma!*, or "A Musical" from *Something Rotten*.

The production number: This usually utilizes the entire cast, the chorus, dancers, and scenery. Examples are "Springtime for Hitler" in *The Producers*, the Ziegfeld Follies extravaganzas, "His Love Makes Me Beautiful" from *Funny Girl*, and *Rent*'s "La Vie Bohème."

The "end of Act One" song: This number wraps up the first act with a bang that leaves the audience on pins and needles, so they come back for the second act. Examples are the "Tonight (Quintet)" from *West Side Story* and "Defying Gravity" from *Wicked*.

The "11 o'clock" number: This is a song that occurs near the end of the second act of a Broadway show (dating back to the old days when the curtain went up at 8:30 p.m.) that brings down the house. Think "Rose's Turn" from *Gypsy*, **"The Music That Makes Me Dance"** from *Funny Girl*, and **"Being Alive"** from *Company*.

BROADER RULES ABOUT MUSICAL THEATER

Make sure it's a marketable idea: I can't tell you how many of my friends spend years on ideas that are not good. I don't have the heart to tell them making Robin Hood as a musical set in Chicago during the twenties isn't a good idea. Use your "gatekeepers" (see chapter 16, p. 115) to make sure what you're writing is commercial and viable in today's marketplace.

Don't do it in a vacuum: Musicals are a collaborative experience. In musical theater, you are always working with at least three people (the cowriter, the book writer, and the director), and usually more. You must learn to compromise, and, more importantly, to recognize the best idea in the room no matter who suggests it. Surround yourself with the best people you can. Never work with someone who's not at least as good as you are.

Capitalize on your successes. After *NBS!*, I realized I had a unique opportunity. The show was a smash, and I had a window of time to write something else for the Celebration Theatre. Since what I had already created was good enough, there was an excellent chance that a second show would be greenlit for production. With composer Shelly Markham (with whom I written the songs for *NBS!*) and a very talented old friend from my seventies songwriters' group, Marie Cain, I wrote a musical revue about getting older in an age-obsessed society. It was called *Too Old for the Chorus (But Not Too Old to be a Star!)*. Director Bob Schrock was also a baby boomer and our songs really resonated with him. Soon, I had two shows at the Celebration, and both were hits!

Make sure you like your collaborators: You're going to be working with these people from two to five years. If they're stubborn or drink too much or live in la-la land I promise that you'll want to kill them far before the show ever opens. Conversely, if they're talented and you get along great, working with them is a never-ending source of joy and inspiration. I'm talking about my collaborators on *Play It Cool*, Marty Cassela and Phil Swann—yes, you guys!

You will rewrite more than you can ever imagine: If you think as a pop writer, you have to rewrite a lot, it's nothing compared to writing for a musical. There are many reasons for this. You do a reading and the song doesn't work, or you change the book and the song doesn't fit like it used to, or the actress playing the character who's singing your song just can't sing it. I remember one day I was in a meeting with the director of the second production of *Too Old for the Chorus* in San Diego and she got all excited because she had an idea of turning one of our songs all around so it basically came from another character's point of view. By this time, my collaborators and I had rewritten most of the songs at least twice, if not three times, and before you could say "Lorenz Hart," we reached into our file and pulled out the exact version she wanted.

You need to know your theater history: Having come into musical theater as a pop writer, I immediately noticed a few differences. People in musical theater know a lot about musical theater. They know who choreographed *Oklahoma!* in 1943 (Agnes DeMille) and the name of the charming number in *Bye Bye Birdie* that didn't become a standard ("This Boy"), and every lyric and detail of Stephen Sondheim's oeuvre. I was fairly good at Broadway 101, but clearly, I had some catching up to do.

Perfect rhymes are still the standard: Twenty years in musical theater have taught me that "imperfect rhymes" are considered "non-rhymes" to a lot of the people I was working with—including my collaborators! As mentioned before, things have loosened up considerably, but the old rules are still there. Don't be surprised if someone acts horrified when you rhyme "girl" with "world"!

And now . . .

My Favorite "Writing for Off Broadway" Story

Composer Phil Swann and I were in New York City doing a reading of our jazz, film-noir musical *Play It Cool*. We were staying at the dilapidated and very old Hotel Pennsylvania near Madison Square Garden. The rooms were the size of postage stamps, but it was autumn in New York, and we were doing our show! Before we flew out, Phil and I had written a very ambitious and rangy song for our lead, and we couldn't wait to hear the actor perform it. During our first musical rehearsal with him, we soon realized that while he was a wonderful actor with a pleasant voice, he was no Mandy Patinkin. The director sent us back to the Hotel Pennsylvania immediately to write a song the actor could sing before our run-through the next day.

Now, I'd always heard of things like that happening in the musical theater world, and here I was with Phil at the Hotel Pennsylvania, in his tiny room with a humongous upright piano taking up all the floor space. To be honest

Poster for the New York production of Play It Cool
(owned by Sharon Rosen, used by permission).

with you, instead of being scared or pressured, I felt just like Oscar Hammerstein II or Yip Harburg, part of a long line of songwriters having to deliver fast in some crummy hotel room. The only place for me to sit was on the bed, and there I was, plopped with my #2 pencil and legal pad until Phil and I came up with one of my favorite songs in the show—the very conversational and narrow-ranged "How Do I Go Home Tonight?" Phil is a great partner in song, and we laughed a lot and just did the work. We came in the next day with the finished number, and the actor sang the song beautifully. It's one of my favorite experiences ever.

Here are the lyrics. By the way, its form is AABA, and the rhymes are perfect. That fits the fifties time period of the show. It's sung by Henry, a closeted, married, gay detective who falls in love with a young singer, Will. I like the hard-boiled film noir jargon near the end.

"How Do I Go Home Tonight?"
Music and lyrics: Mark Winkler and Phil Swann (Used with Permission)

How do I go home tonight?
How do I just pretend?
How can I win? When all my cards are in plain sight,
How do I go home tonight?

How do I walk thru the door?
See her face and say hello.
How do I deal? Keep the conversation real and light.
How do I go home tonight?

Everything I want is here,
Everything I have is there.
Isn't it strange, how quickly things can change,
Quickly, but not so clear.

How do I go home tonight?
To someplace where I don't belong.
Tell me where to start?
It's murder on my heart.
This tough guy's not so smart, that's right.
How do I go home tonight?

Robyn Hurder in the New York production of Play It Cool. *What a dress! (Photo by Joan Marcus. Used by Permission.)*

Have a clear idea of the show's theme: I've heard that for every Disney animated musical, there is a sign on the wall of the writers' office that explains the theme of the musical. It's a good reminder to help the songwriters stay focused. For example, *Beauty and the Beast*'s theme is "Don't Judge a Book by Its Cover."

Live in either New York, L.A., Chicago, Minneapolis, Toronto, or London: Yes, there is great theater being done all over the world, but the greatest concentration of talent and opportunity is in these six cities, and most definitely in New York.

Last but not least—have a thick skin. It's tough out there. Show business is exciting and glamorous and more fun than just about anything in life could ever be, but it has another side. It can be hard and unfair and humiliate you very publicly (social media anyone?). *Naked Boys Singing!* was charmed from the very beginning—great reviews, sold-out shows, the whole works. However, *Play It Cool*, for which I wrote all the lyrics, had a more twisted path. It started out in L.A. at Celebration Theatre and was also a hit with great reviews and full audiences. However, though the critics uniformly loved the musical numbers, quite a few said the book needed some work. Nevertheless, they liked the adventurous gay subject matter, which in 2006 was a little daring and ahead of its time.

The show got away with being somewhat preachy and expository because every time the pace lagged, there were two bare-chested guys kissing or a great musical number. When *Play It Cool* opened Off Broadway five years later, the world had moved fast on the whole gay issue. The TV show *Glee* regularly showed two guys kissing and same-sex marriage was legal in many states. With *Will and Grace* and *Ellen*, people were just more comfortable with the whole LGBTQ thing. And though we'd improved the book, the show was still pontificating in places.

By opening night, I had been in Midtown Manhattan for a whole month of rehearsals. I always think of this period as, "It was the best of times; it was the worst of times."

The best of times: the first preview performance at the Acorn Theatre on 42nd Street was preceded by hellacious tech rehearsals, which can suck the energy out of anyone. The audience loved the show and the standing ovation was led by my husband, Richard Del Belso, who had flown in that day.

The worst of times: New York critics don't come on opening night. They came to the previews in the two days leading up to the opening. For the Saturday matinee before the opening, we had a whole row of ladies and gentlemen of the press sitting there with their arms folded in front of their chests, daring our little show to be good. I recognized the critic John Simon, whose reviews are known for being eviscerating, and the expression on his face was all that and a bag of chips—before the show even started. He scared me so much I had to leave the theater and I didn't come back until the intermission.

Okay, back to opening night. Tovah Feldshuh was there, flirted with me, and loved the show. However, I was numb, that's about all I remember. When the opening night party was over, Richard and I went back to our hotel room and awaited the online reviews that were all going to be coming in a little after midnight.

The reviews were finally posted and ouch, they weren't good; they were rather awful. Though the critics liked the music and my lyrics generally—and loved Sally Mayes's knockout performance in the lead role—they had a lot of trouble with the book and its preachy, expository nature. As each review appeared, I noticed that my left hand (I'm left-handed) started shaking. And I felt like if I saw one more bad review I was going to have a heart attack.

Get a life!: Don't be so consumed with your career that you have nothing else to define you other than your work. It took me a long time to figure this out, but by 2011 I was in a wonderful thirty-year relationship, and it saved me at one of the lowest points in my career.

Here I am getting pummeled with bad reviews online at midnight—so what did I do? I closed my laptop, held on to my wonderful partner Richard, and went to bed. How was I so smart to save myself hours of beating myself with a wet bamboo stick, reading and rereading the bad reviews? I guess I was old enough to value myself and my emotional well-being over the show. It turned out *The New York Times* review would be coming out on Monday—three days away. However, instead of waiting for it to come, we had planned a trip to Washington, DC, to get out of town and have a little fun! And that's just what we did.

The Associated Press review was wonderful, but, alas, *The New York Ttimes* review (written by a newbie critic who had opined about architecture until just the week before) was bad. However, even worse, she didn't know anything about film noir, and so didn't understand why the guy in the trench coat kept narrating the whole thing. I guess she'd never seen a Humphrey Bogart film either.

My last musical theater tip and major life lesson: I never accept what critics, or friends, or the public say about my work. I do, ultimately, ask myself, "Hey, Mark. What did you think?" Now that time has passed and I find myself smiling whenever I look at the *Play It Cool* poster hanging on the wall next to my bed, I'm proud of that show. The level of mastery of the lighting designer, the set designer, the choreographer, and the singing and acting were just amazing. It was a first-class production. And I made lifelong friends of our wonderful director Sharon Rosen, cowriter Phil Swann, and the book writer of record, Marty Casella. And the cherry on top of the cake was a wonderful evening performing at 54 Below with our Outer Critics Circle Award-nominated star, Sally Mayes. Love her.

I do not mean to dismiss outside reality. The bad reviews closed *Play It Cool*. However, I've seen too many of my colleagues go with what the latest person has said about their work, rather than reach into their gut and trust their own feelings. That kind of second-guessing can drive you crazy and lead you to inferior work. Personally, I think *Play It Cool* is terrific. The songs are among my best, the characters in the show are indelible, and it's a fascinating look into what it was like to be gay in the fifties.

A friend and wonderful lyricist/singer, Lorraine Feather, once gave me a book called *Lexicon of Musical Invective: Critical Assaults on Composers Since Beethoven's Time* by Nicolas Slonimsky. In it, you can find critics calling F. Scott Fitzgerald's *The Great Gatsby* a disappointment and Gershwin's *Porgy and Bess* terrible. Sometimes critics and gatekeepers and the times we live in are wrong. It's always good to check in on what you think, and that goes both ways. There are songs of mine a lot of people like that I'm not particularly crazy about. However, I'm not telling anyone that!

To wrap this all up, I love musical theater. As a songwriter, it's a great venue for artistic and monetary fulfillment. Live theater is never going to be replaced by the internet, and Stephen Schwartz and Lin-Manuel Miranda are raking in the money. As for me, after *Play It Cool*, I went on to be a co-writer on *Bark! The Musical* (a celebration of all things dog that has been quite successful and played all over the country) and *Something's Got to Give* (a musical about Marilyn Monroe), which has never been produced (book problems!). And I'm eager to get back to writing a new show. I think I have a very good idea, which I'm keeping close to my vest at this moment.

SONGWRITING ACTIONS

Okay, write an "I want" song for your musical. What? You haven't got a musical yet? No worries. Even though you see yourself at this moment as just a writer or performer, writing musicals is something you should consider. If you're successful, it's very lucrative and, take my word for it, there's nothing quite like hearing your songs sung by an incredible Broadway professional to a very enthusiastic full house.

I'm picking a movie for you: watch the movie and then write your "I Want" song for it. The movie I've chosen is *King Richard*, which is the story of Serena and Venus Williams's father, Richard Williams. When I was watching this fascinating movie, starring Will Smith, I kept thinking, What does this movie remind me of? A desperate-yet-charming parent working with two of his young children to make them stars and share in their glory, and ultimately overreaching a little bit. Then, it came to me—Mama Rose and *Gypsy*. Same plot!!

1. Watch the movie or read the book *King Richard*. You won't be sorry.
2. Who's singing? (*The father Richard.*) Who is he singing to? (*To his daughters, to his wife, to the world—you pick.*) What is he trying to accomplish, what does he want? (*He wants it all!! To let the whole world know Serena and Venus Williams, though economically challenged girls from Compton, are going to be the greatest tennis stars in the history of the sport.*)
3. What's the tone of the song? (*Optimistic, driving, a little desperate.*)
4. What is the style of the music? (*The movie is set in the eighties and they're in Compton, but Richard rejects his environment somewhat, so when he's singing—no rap. I'd say old school R&B, the kind the father would listen to. Maybe even a little Motown thrown in for good measure, or perhaps some Ashford and Simpson.*)
5. Use the father's particular dialect to inform the tune. He's from the South and while he's obviously smart, he's not school smart, so his grammar isn't that good.
6. Because it's Broadway, use masculine, feminine, three rhymes, and inner rhyming. Craft is of the utmost importance on the Broadway stage.

Look at all the information you've got to start with—and notice it's exactly the same information you need to write a good pop song. When I write a song for a character in one of my musicals, I become that character—you have the movie and the book to tell you a lot about *King Richard*—now write it.

OBJECTIVES OF THE SONGWRITING ACTIONS:
- To write an "I want song" for a Broadway musical.
- To use all the tools of commercial songwriting to shape a lyric for a specific character to sing in a musical that will further the story along by showing the audience what the character wants.

18
STRATEGIES FOR CREATING NEW SONGS

Sometimes, we as songwriters—especially singer/songwriters—write too many songs of a particular type. For example, songwriters and singers are overly fond of ballads written about unrequited love (okay, I don't mean to be picking on *you*). Too much of even a good thing can be boring. And in terms of a live performance, it's not what the doctor ordered. To show your range as a songwriter, it's great to have a variety of songs that you're good at. The Beatles, Ed Sheeran, Bruno Mars, and Taylor Swift wrote incredible songs, different kinds of songs with different topics, different rhythms, and different points of view.

Bruno Mars
"Uptown Funk" (eighties R&B dance number)
"The Lazy Song" (comedic reggae song)
"When I Was Your Man" (straight-out love ballad)
"That's What I Like" (retro R&B crooner)
"Locked Out of Heaven" (ska meets The Police)

The Beatles
"Michelle" (lovely guitar ballad with a few French lyrics)
"Helter Skelter" (heavy rock song)
"When I'm Sixty-Four" (vaudeville shuffle)

"A Day in the Life" (ambitious mash-up of at least two songs)
"Yesterday" (classic AABA Great American Songbook song)
"She Loves You" (midtempo rock song)
"Revolution 9" (sound collage)
"Tomorrow Never Knows" and "Lucy in the Sky with Diamonds" (psychedelic rock)

Taylor Swift
"I Knew You Were Trouble" (straight-ahead pop song)
"Shake It Off" (up-tempo, personal, self-empowerment anthem)
"Blank Space" (lyrics that play on fans' fantasies)
"Mean" (country message song)
"Style" (eighties electro-pop vibe)
"Me" (power pop)
"Betty" (folksy story song)

Ed Sheeran
"Perfect" (classic love song à la Phil Collins)
"Galway Girl" (Irish jig)
"The Shape of You" (rap-influenced verses married to a pop chorus)
"A-Team" (guitar-driven story song)
"Supermarket Flowers" (sensitive piano ballad)

So, how do you get some variety into your songwriting? Here are some proven types of songs that might fill in some holes in your songbook.

CHARACTER SONGS
A character song: a genre that can define the singer as an artist and a person. You'll find them to be part of most singer/songwriters' repertoire.

Jennifer Lopez: "Jenny from the Block"
The Allman Brothers: "Ramblin' Man"
Lin-Manuel Miranda "Alexander Hamilton" (from the musical, *Hamilton*)
James Taylor: "Sweet Baby James"
Barbra Streisand: "I'm the Greatest Star"
Dolly Parton: "Coat of Many Colors"

STRATEGIES FOR CREATING NEW SONGS

Loretta Lynn: "Coal Miner's Daughter"
Tina Turner: "Private Dancer"
Eminem: "The Real Slim Shady"
Prince: "Baby I'm a Star"
Pink: "Don't Let Me Get Me"
Bruce Springsteen: "Born in the U.S.A."

Here's a character song from one of my best students. Almost every line is full of specificity, strong emotion, and a lovely poetic tone:

"The Collector"
Lyrics by Amy Vandivort (Used with Permission)

Verse #1
There's a woman who owns an antique shop on eighth street,
She has old clocks and end tables and a box of unopened memories,
> *Winkler: Love how specific this phrase is: not just that she has things, but she names them and then at the end she gets poetic with "unopened memories"*

And there's an entire room of chairs where no one ever takes a seat,
It's my favorite place in this city.
> *Strong emotional line*

Verse #2
I see a little of myself in this woman or maybe I see her in me,
Or maybe it's just the antique mirrors where I see myself most clearly.
> *Specific item with a poetic twist at end of line*

Every time I visit, she's got another new old thing.
> *Nice word play and uses opposites*

Every time I come in, I've got another piece of my identity.

Chorus
I'm collecting pieces of who I should be.
> *Strong emotional line that tells you whole plot in one sentence—whew!*

I pick each one up indiscriminately,

From women who are much more impressive than me,
I'm just a collector, don't mind me.
> She puts the title in a lovely, self-effacing way

Then there are character songs written from the third person's perspective, where they talk about a character who is not them.

Kenny Rogers: "The Gambler"
Ed Sheeran: "The A Team"
Lady Gaga: "Joanne"
Elton John: "Goodbye Norma Jean (Candle in the Wind)"
Curtis Mayfield: "Freddie's Dead"
Isaac Hayes: "Shaft"
Fugees with Lauren Hill: "Killing Me Softly with His Song"
Tanya Tucker, Helen Reddy, and Bette Midler's recordings of "Delta Dawn"
Chuck Berry: "Johnny B. Goode"
Sting: "Roxanne"

Winkler digresses . . .
When Faith Hill was the queen of pretty-girl country pop, Gretchen Wilson came along as Hill's worst nightmare with "Redneck Woman." Pink did the same thing when Britney Spears was the top in pop and literally said she was the anti-Britney with "Don't Let Me Get Me."

LOCATION SONGS
There are songs with a sense of place. I call them "location songs." Writing a location song is always fun because the location gives you so many details with which to work. Think of writing a location song about . . .

- Your hometown
- A haunted house
- A deserted amusement park
- A cruise to Alaska
- Your favorite or least favorite city
- The moon
- Las Vegas
- On the road as a famous singer

Here are some great examples of location songs:

Weezer: "Beverly Hills"
Katy Perry: "California Girls"
Joni Mitchell: "Carey"
The Chainsmokers: "Paris"
Miley Cyrus: "Malibu"
Billy Joel: "Piano Man"
Frank Sinatra: "New York, New York"
Jay Z and Alicia Keys: "Empire State of Mind"
Randy Newman: "Louisiana," "Baltimore," and "I Love L.A."
Taylor Swift: "Welcome to New York"
The Beatles: "Penny Lane"
Chris Stapleton: "Midnight Train to Memphis"
Post Malone: "Hollywood's Bleeding"
The Kinks: "Celluloid Heroes"
Tony Bennett: "I Left My Heart in San Francisco"
Leonard Cohen: "First We Take Manhattan"
The B-52s: "Love Shack"

Here's an evocative location song, "California," by my student Julie Logue. I think I like it so much because the specifics in the song really give you a feel for what it must be like to be in this very interesting state. By the way, the first line of her chorus, "I bet that heaven looks like California," is a great hook—so catchy and memorable. I'm just including the chorus and the bridge of this song; they seem to have the juiciest writing in them.

"California"
Lyrics by Julie Logue (Used with Permission)

Chorus
I bet that heaven looks like California.
   Winkler: Very catchy phrase that tells you the story of the song in one line
I bet the sun shines bright as the Golden Gate.
   Specific image true to California
Like a sunset drive along the coastal line,
   Another specific image

I bet that it takes your breath away.
I bet heaven looks like California.

Bridge
Like a redwood in the sky,
> *Every image screams out California!!*

Or an ocean wave at night.
A canyon road in Calabasas,
A palm tree in the wind,
Santa Anas pull you in . . .

Here's an even more specific location song from my student Heather Perram Frank about a location on the other side of the country. In terms of location, she really nails the different cities the train is going through, and my favorite location specificity is "South of '95 near the Maryland state line."

"Red Toad Road"
Lyrics by Heather Perram Frank (Used with Permission)

Verse #1
Racing through the station to catch the 2:05,
> *Winkler: Nice specific picture—very specific to the second*

I just hope you're waiting when I finally arrive.
Give my roller to the Red Cap so I can get on fast,
> *Love this! Alliteration and uber specificity*

Two hours 'til I know if you're my future or my past.
> *The stakes are high! She's got a ticking clock! Two good things to do in a story**

Chorus
Almost, almost, I'm almost there,
Please be waiting when I get to Delaware.
> *She nails the location*

God, don't let it be our final episode,
I just want to be with you on Red Toad Road.
> *Strong emotional line and specific location that just happens to be title of the tune*

*It's always great to make your stakes high in a song. It's never just a "nice" date, but a "fabulous date" or a date that changed your life. Strong emotions are called for in songs. The ticking time clock is used in screenplays all the time and it adds urgency to your song. You've got to complete an action and you have a specified time to do it. It heightens the drama.

KINDS OF SONGS

So, we all know there are love songs; songs about when you fall in love, fall out of love, unrequited love. And to be honest, most hit songs are love songs in some way. But sometimes a hit song can be a *philosophy song*, a song that talks about the meaning of life. My favorite one is a song that I happened to be in on when it was created.

Winkler digresses . . .

As I've already mentioned, I was in a songwriting group in the late seventies into the eighties that met every Monday night for at least six years and there were some wonderful songwriters in it. The leader and grande dame of the group was a fabulous lyricist named Phyllis Molinary. One night, she told us she had started writing a song, "Here's to Life," with famed songwriter Artie Butler (another friend of mine). The following week she came in and sang it and it was amazing! The next time I heard about it, Phyllis excitedly told me that the great jazz singer Joe Williams had fallen in love with the tune and was going to record it. He went on The Tonight Show Starring Johnny Carson *and sang it beautifully.*

Shirley Horn, another great jazz singer, heard it that night and decided to record it. She was going into the studio, with Johnny Mandel arranging. Joe Williams found out about this and rushed to record it with the London Philharmonic Orchestra, and then another curious thing happened: when Joe got to the session, the song, arranged for a large symphony orchestra, was in the wrong key. Joe sang it well in the higher key, but it did rob his version of some of the intimacy of the tune. Joe was crestfallen.

Shirley Horn recorded it in the perfect key with a perfect arrangement. "Here's to Life" became her theme song and a jazz classic that won Johnny Mandel a GRAMMY for his arrangement. Since then, it seems every singer in the world has recorded it, from Barbra Streisand to Michael Feinstein. I was with Phyllis at the hospital shortly before she died (much too young) and together we watched Barbra's TV special at the Village Vanguard. When she sang, "Here's to Life," I remember Phyllis gripping my hand and giving me a look that said, "Okay, this is about as good as it gets for a songwriter." A lovely memory. When Phyllis passed, her daughter gave me her rhyming dictionary and it is cherished.

I think of this as a perfect song. It can fit almost any occasion and is so rooted in emotion that it is impossible not to feel it. I finally recorded "Here's to Life" on my album, *The Company I Keep*. Here's the wonderful lyric:

"Here's to Life"
Lyrics by Phyllis Molinary (Used with Permission)

Verse 1
No complaints and no regrets,
  Winkler: Short phrases filled with feeling
I still believe in chasing dreams and placing bets,
And I have learned that all you give is all you get,
  This repetition of "all you" is an anaphora
So give it all you got.
  She repeats "give it all you" again

Verse 2
I had my share, I drank my fill,
And even though I'm satisfied I'm hungry still,
  Opposites work great in songs, "drank my fill, hungry still"
To see what's down another road beyond a hill,
And do it all again.

Chorus
So, here's to life,
And all the joy it brings.
Here's to life,
To dreamers and their dreams.
  Nice alliteration for the payoff line or stinger

STRATEGIES FOR CREATING NEW SONGS

Verse 3

Funny how the time just flies,
> *Nice alliteration—"funny" and "flies"*

How love can go from warm hellos to sad goodbyes,
> *Opposites again*

And leave you with the memories you've memorized,
> *One great alliteration!*

To keep your winters warm.

Verse 4

Cause there's no yes in yesterday,
> *What a clever and heavily emotional line. Could be a song title on its own*

And who knows what tomorrow brings or takes away,

As long as I'm still in the game I wanna play,
> *Emotional declaration of singer's intent*

For laughs, for life, for love.
> *Alliteration again!*

Chorus

So, here's to life,
And all the joy it brings,
So, here's to life,
To dreamers and their dreams.

Post-chorus

May all your storms be weathered,
And all that's good get better.
Here's to life, Here's to love, Here's to you.

Here are some other great versions of *philosophy* songs:

"Fight Song" as sung by Rachel Patton
"What a Wonderful World" as sung by Louis Armstrong
"Fireworks" as sung by Katy Perry

"And When I Die" as sung by Laura Nyro
"Live Like You're Dying" as sung by Tim McGraw
"Humble and Kind" as sung by Tim McGraw

And finally, I come to a category of song: "the message song." A message song is very close to a philosophy song, but a message song generally tries to address an injustice in the world, while a philosophy song can just be a contemplation on life.

Every year I have an idealistic student who wants to change the world with their songs. And often, their attempts are off the mark. They're preachy and hard core, sometimes deprecating their audience.

Or in Suzanne Vega's heartbreaking song about child abuse, "Luka," which is told from the viewpoint of the abused child who spends half of the song blaming himself and letting his family off the hook. Powerful stuff.

In Macklemore and Ryan's "Same Love," Macklemore sings that when he was a little boy, everybody thought he was gay. And then he talks about the love between his two gay "Uncles." This song never feels preachy, because the singer is talking about his reality and his opinions.

And, finally, there's the Randy Newman song, "Sail Away," which talks about the horror of slavery. His brilliance as a writer is that he shows it all through the eyes of the captain of the slave ship spinning lies to his Black captives about how wonderful it's going to be for them in America.

So, when you write your message song, and you all will:

- Keep it specific
- Be nonjudgmental
- Find a way into it that is unique and surprising
- Don't be on the nose. For example, don't just "tell" us not to buy grapes because of the poor working conditions of the migrant workers. In your lyric, perhaps become a migrant worker and then "show" the problem through their eyes. Maybe even become a grape who feels terrible that it's being picked to profit the big bosses of industry! Be audacious—get into the thick of the emotion. Don't stand back and tell me what's wrong. Jump in!
- Use all your technique and craft to make it come alive for the listener
- And, good luck

Here are other powerful message songs:

"Ballad of the Hurricane," "Masters of War," "Maggie's Farm," "Blowin' in the Wind," and "Serve Somebody" as sung by Bob Dylan
"Strange Fruit" as sung by Billie Holiday
"Hello in There" as sung by John Prine
"Big Yellow Taxi" as sung by Joni Mitchell
"Ghost Town" by as sung by The Specials
"This Is America" as sung by Childish Gambino
"Killing in the Name" as sung by Rage Against the Machine
"Fortunate Son" as sung by John Fogerty and Creedence Clearwater Revival
"Pride (In the Name of Love)" and "Sunday Bloody Sunday" as sung by U2

SONGWRITING ACTIONS

To help you bring variety to your songs, write either a *character*, *location*, or *message* song.

OBJECTIVES OF THE SONGWRITING ACTIONS

To allow you to investigate types of songs you have not previously written before. Plus, to expand your vocabulary as a songwriter and broaden your range.

19
SHOW, DON'T TELL

I once saw a play about Lena Horne, the great singer and actress of the forties and fifties, best known for singing "Stormy Weather" and her fantastic one-woman show *Lena Horne: The Lady and Her Music*. Horne was an amazingly talented trailblazer who led a fascinating life, so why was I getting more and more irritated with the play, and even her?

It all came down to too much "telling" and too little "showing."

To explain: there's a scene in the play where her grown-up son comes to visit her and before she can even usher him into her quite lovely New York penthouse, he bellows, "Mom, I'm an alcoholic and I'll never be anything but an alcoholic." And then Lena reiterates what her son just told her (in case somebody left the theater in the last two minutes) and adds, "You're breaking my heart." Tell, tell, tell.

How much better would it have been, if, when she opened the door to let her son into her penthouse, he had his jacket buttoned unevenly, a sloppy smirk on his face, and while stepping into her sunken living room, he grew unsteady on his feet, tripped, and subsequently fell on the floor (maybe having a little bottle fall out of his pocket)? Melodramatic to be sure, but "showing" is always the better and more engaging thing to do.

The same approach applies in songwriting. When you tell your listener what's going on, they then can't discover it themselves. Audiences love to discover the clues and where the plots are going—it's what they do in real life. And in songwriting, that goes double. It's actions that reveal character and plot and emotions.

Once again, like a broken record, I reiterate that you can never lose as a lyricist by "showing" the scene, how the characters are feeling and what is happening, and, naturally, the more specific the better.

SHOW DON'T TELL PARAGRAPH

Here's a little exercise I enjoy doing with my class.

Write a first-person perspective paragraph. It does not have to rhyme or adhere to any songwriting form—it's just a paragraph.

You need to show:

1. To whom are you singing?
2. You're in a relationship. What just happened between you and the other person?
3. How do you feel about it?
4. Where are you?
5. What time is it?
6. What do you want to accomplish by writing the paragraph?

If you're Mike Posner, in one of my favorite songs of the last few years, "I Took a Pill in Ibiza," this is how you'd answer the questions:

1. I'm singing to naive singer/songwriters who think I'm pretty hot shit.
2. The naive singer/songwriters think I'm great because I've had one or two hits, but I know I'm washed-up.
3. I'm sad, yet philosophical about it all.
4. Anyplace where a random fan would start talking to me.
5. It feels like the midnight of my soul.
6. A cautionary tale to warn would-be singer/songwriters not to do what I did.

Check out the lyrics of this song online; it made him a "two-hit wonder" and was nominated for Song of the Year at the GRAMMYS. To find the lyrics go to: https://genius.com/Mike-posner-i-took-a-pill-in-ibiza-lyrics.

Or if you were Tom Douglas and Allen Shamblin, who wrote Miranda Lambert's "The House That Built Me," here's what their answers would look like:

1. She's singing to the current owner of her childhood home
2. She's reminiscing about life with her family in their house
3. She's nostalgic, and glad to be "home" after having her confidence shaken
4. Standing at the front door
5. Daytime
6. Remembering who she is and where she came from gives her strength and courage to face the world again

Allen Shamblin and Tom Douglas didn't ever tell us this—they "showed" it to us in detail. Check out the lyrics online and see how the song is like a little movie. In fact, the lyrics made a great shooting script for the poignant music video. To find the lyrics go to: https://genius.com/Miranda-lambert-the-house-that-built-me-lyrics.

And if you're Madonna (with cowriter Brian Elliott) in "Papa Don't Preach," here's how you'd answer the questions:

1. I'm an unmarried young girl singing to my father
2. I'm confessing to Dad that I'm pregnant
3. I'm defiant, defensive, and a little nervous
4. In the living room of the family house
5. When my father is home from work
6. To convince my dad to help me and accept the baby I want to keep

Check out the lyrics to this song; it's early Madonna but well written and quite unusual. To find the lyrics go to: https://genius.com/Madonna-papa-dont-preach-lyrics.

Here are two examples from my talented students who completed "The Show Don't Tell Paragraph" exercise earlier in the chapter.

Thelma Valenzuela (Used with Permission):

1. To whom are you singing? *My husband*
2. What just happened between you two? *We just had a big argument*

3. How do you feel about it? *Angry and sad*
4. Where are you? *Home*
5. What time is it? *Late at night*
6. What do you want to accomplish by writing the paragraph? *Make him understand that I'm angry but that doesn't mean I don't love him*

The room falls into familiar silence, after the ticking time bomb I set off in you. You storm off to your corner of the room and scroll angrily through a phone that you once used to send me sweet messages, while I go sit next to our little dog and find comfort in giving her soft pats. (These fights have become so routine; they don't even faze me anymore.) I look up at you, willing you to return my gaze, hoping that you still see the love I have for you through my tears. You look up and give me a sad knowing smile. I get ready for bed.

Mark Gavotos (Used with Permission):

1. To whom are you singing? *An old high school bandmate*
2. What just happened between you two? *We just sat down for a drink*
3. How do you feel about it? *Nostalgic*
4. Where are you? *Our high school reunion*
5. What time is it? *Cocktail hour*
6. What do you want to accomplish by writing the paragraph? *Tell my friend that I miss the old days and that I wish I could jam one more time*

Hey Johnny! It's great to see you again after twenty years. We may be a little broader around the middle and thinner on the top, but I remember the days when the Mighty Snacks rocked these high school walls with songs by Springsteen and the Eagles—with me on my Mustang Bass and you on your seafoam-green Strat. We ruled the world when we played rock 'n' roll, my friend, and since the evening is still young, I say we get another Jim Beam, find the other snacks, and show these alumni that we still got something left in the tank. Are you with me, bro?

SONGWRITING ACTIONS

So now it's your turn to answer the questions I posed at the beginning of the lesson and write the paragraph. Do it in ten minutes. And remember, you can't *tell* these things—you have to *show* them!

I'm not saying never to "tell" in a song—some great songs do a little of that. I'm just saying always try to "show" the scene.

Don't *tell* "I'm feeling blue cause you left me."
Show it in words.

Don't *tell* "I'm in love and feeling great."
Show it.

Don't *tell* "I'm so mad, I feel like I'm going to explode."
Show it.

We all have "gifts" in songwriting, and the more you write, the more you're going to realize what comes naturally to you, and what you need to work on a bit. When I was in high school, I was in an a cappella choir and art classes. Truthfully, I got more recognition for my art. I won numerous prizes with my woodblock prints and drawings and even a scholarship to Los Angeles' Art Center. So, I've always been a visual writer—it's my little "gift." I'm not the funniest writer (I learned that while writing musicals with a very funny lady, Marie Cain) and I'm not the most dexterous rhymer in the world. However, visually, I can fly! Recently, I was struck by how many excellent lyricists are also fine artists like Joni Mitchell and Bob Dylan (yes, Bob Dylan), David Bowie, Stevie Nicks, Kurt Cobain, and Marilyn Manson, to just name a few.

Here's one of my most visual songs.

Your Cat Plays Piano
Lyrics by Mark Winkler

Verse 1
There's so many things about you baby I like,
   Winkler: Very conversational

For example, when you wake up and say "Good mornin',"
> *Its like a scene in a movie—the line defines her character*

About a quarter to midnight.
And I got this thing for your dancin' eyes,
I can't tell a lie, it's the way I feel so cool with you,
When we're all alone and the moon is high,
But the thing I like the most
Is when . . .

Chorus
Your cat plays piano,
> *Unique picture*

Mostly on the black keys,
And I could swear he's a jazzer,
> *Insider dig on jazz musicians*

'Cause he will not play the melody.
When your cat plays piano,
And I hear you singin' along,
> *Once again showing how kooky this girl is—very cinematic*

It's all so amazing,
How you seem to know just every little note to his song.

Verse 2
And as for your funky little pad, what's not to like?
I'm hip to your collection of records playin' on the old hi-fi.
> *She's retro and attracted to hipster stuff*

And I'm mad for your abstracts, though I can't seem to understand,
> *The singer telling us the girl is cooler and more mysterious than he is*

Why you've got this collection of Slinkys on the green nightstand.
And though I can't say what your poetry's about,
> *Once again showing the singer is a little bit out of his depth with the girl*

I know it's very deep, never know just what you're gonna do,
When the incense burns and the scarves come out,
> *Strong imagery, involves our sense of smell and sight*

But the thing I like the most
Is when . . .

Chorus
Your cat plays piano,
Livin' out his nine lives,
   Associative phrase to cats
Like Monk or Mr. Parker,
Although I hear some Charles Ives.
   Now the singer shows he's a little "out" too
When your cat plays piano,
And I hear you singing along,
It's all so amazing,
How you seem to know just every little note to his song.

20

WRITE A SONG LIKE A MOVIE

Some things in songs always work. And putting pictures into your songs is one of them.

A picture is worth a thousand words, and somehow a verbal picture has that rare ability to immediately put you into the scene where the song is taking place and showing, rather than telling you, the emotions your characters are experiencing. There's no way you can lose if you channel Steven Spielberg and direct a little movie the next time you write a song.

Sometimes, I find that beginning songwriters' songs are devoid of "pictures" and, therefore, are just strings of words. Often, there's no repetition, the title is uninvolving and doesn't capture what the song is about. However, if you make your song like a movie, you'll naturally add the "furniture" that will make it stand out.

The song "Jesus, Take the Wheel" was Carrie Underwood's first hit after winning *American Idol* and the first one of her multitude of number one songs in her career.

It went to number one on the country chart and became a Top 20 hit on the *Billboard* Hot 100. Written by Hillary Lindsey, Gordie Sampson, and Brett James, it won Single of the Year at the GRAMMYS in 2005 and is certified three-times platinum by RIAA. It is one of her best songs. The first verse is like watching the first ten minutes of a really good movie.

To find the lyrics go to: https://genius.com/Carrie-underwood-jesus-take-the-wheel-lyrics.

Here's another one of my favorites: Marc Cohen's classic song, "Walking in Memphis." It's like you are the camera recording the action, and it's all "show" and very little "tell."

To find the lyrics go to https://genius.com/Marc-cohn-walking-in-memphis-lyrics.

Winkler digresses . . .

When I was seventeen, I came to a fork in my career path. Although I came from a family of singers and sang continually around the house, I also excelled in high school as a visual artist.

After high school, I enrolled at Cal Arts, intending to major in commercial art. However, I was also singing with bands on the weekends and working with my mentor, Jimmie Haskell, on different song projects. I kept dropping out more and more from college to sing and rehearse my music, and, in that way, music somewhat chose me.

Luckily, I never lost my love of imagery and continue to make good use of it in my lyrics. I love being a painter and showing the scene; it's a gift I have. The more you write the more you discover what your gifts are.

Here's a lyric I wrote that turned out to be the title song for my album, *Ebony Rain*. It came to me when I was vacationing in what I think is one of the most magical places in the world, Kaua'i, one of the islands of Hawai'i. My husband and I were sightseeing, when down from the sky came this dark ash dappling our shoulders and heads and every other surface with a dark dust. When we asked what it was, our tour guides said it was what happened when the farmers burned the sugarcane while processing it. I immediately thought it was a dynamite metaphor for making love in a tropical place. Here's the lyrics:

Ebony Rain

produced by
DAVID BENOIT · EDDIE ARKIN

featuring
DIANNE REEVES · TOM SCOTT

Mark's second album Ebony Rain (album art owned by Mark Winkler).

"Ebony Rain"
Lyrics by Mark Winkler

Verse #1
It's a ramshackle town,
A tourist's delight—it's a soft Hawaiian night.
You were standing on the balcony,
   Winkler: Like a scene in a movie, tourist comes to island and sees girl
Just above the street,

Like a Gauguin in the light,
All primitive and wild,
There were secrets you weren't telling,
Hidden in your smile.

Verse #2
I'd come to see the islands,
With a suitcase full of blues,
A restless heart to lose,
And behind the rusted grillwork,
   Very visual lines as the camera pans in
Near a bamboo-shaded room,
You beckoned me to you,
With fire in your eyes.
I guess I took my chances,
For this chance at paradise.

Chorus
They're burning down the green fields,
   Every line is like another scene in the movie, serving as a metaphor for their love
For the sugar cane [*sic*],
Cinders and ash are pourin' down,
Like ebony rain.
Volcanoes lay waitin' for another day,
Palm trees are swaying in the spell,
Of ebony rain, ebony rain.

Verse #3
The ceiling fan keeps busy,
   A scene a little later in the movie, the love has progressed
Turnin' round above our heads,
Throwing shadows on the bed.
You feed me sweet papaya,
Bits of passion fruit,
Like a hungry little kid,

All the juices running down,
We're lovers in the moonlight,
In this enchanted town.

Winkler digresses just once more . . .

When Phil Swann and I were writing Play It Cool, our musical that wound up playing Off Broadway, our lead character Mary was a lesbian who ran an underground jazz club in L.A. In 1953, it was very much against the law to be gay in a bar with other gays.

But, in the show, the writer of the book always had Mary dressed in a sharp suit, with her hair slicked back, looking like a man. Mary was nobody's fool, she also knew that in Los Angeles at that time they had a rule that if you were in a bar and you were a woman, you could skirt around the law by having three items of women's clothing on you . . . and she did. Although, we as the audience did not know what they were specifically.

After we had our first workshop, one thing became very clear to me. I had to give Mary a backstory explaining why she dressed in "drag," and it was one of my favorite experiences. And this speaks to the magic of writing songs and being in the theater, which is all show-and-tell. I merged my empathy for Mary with my particular perspective as a gay man. I've never worn drag, but plenty of gay and straight men wear women's clothes for a variety of reasons. I just needed to locate Mary's reason for wearing drag and was home free. The two actresses who played Mary both brought down the house with this song, which is like a movie with flashbacks.

In My Drag
Lyrics by Mark Winkler

Verse #1
Once upon a straight old time,
I was a cute little wifey-poo,
> *Winkler: The first lines sets the tone, which is sort of self-effacing and humorous*

Married to this handsome hunk,
Who liked to beat me black and blue.
> *Once again just throwing off this line*

Verse #2
Dressin' in the nicest threads,
He went to work sellin' beds all day,
Leavin' wifey-poo alone,
Just to waste away.

Pre-chorus
I used to wait till the man was gone,
    Now we have a scene in the movie—and it plays out
Then slip into his slacks,
Put on his shirt and his underwear,
Smoke his stogies and just relax.

Chorus
In my drag,
Feelin' confident,
In my drag,
Is where I'd invent,
An alter-ego with the golden touch,
Big and strong—I never needed much,
In my drag,
In my drag,
In my drag.

Verse #3
In a year or less
The light at our address had lost its glow,
(Don't you know).
'Til he walked through the door,
    Now another scene in our little movie unfolds
And found his baby dressed like "daddy-o."

Verse #4
He said, "Who are you, Jack?
I want my wifey back,"
But I said, "no!

You haven't got a chance,
I like to wear the pants,"
And I turned to go.

Pre-chorus
He raised his hand and said, "I'm the boss,"
His pretty smile suffered quite a loss,
I beat that man with his walkin' stick,
Yes, I turned the tables on that little prick.

Here are some other songs that are like movies:

"Hotel California" as sung by the Eagles
"U and Ur Hand" as sung by Pink
"Moves Like Jagger" as sung by Maroon 5
"Last Friday Night" and "Teenage Dream" as sung by Katy Perry
"Norwegian Wood," "She's Leaving Home," and "Penny Lane" as sung by The Beatles
"Castle on the Hill" as sung by Ed Sheeran
"One for My Baby" as sung by Frank Sinatra
"Ode to Billie Joe" as sung by Bobbie Gentry
"Strawberry Wine" as sung by Deana Carter
"Fancy" as sung by Reba McIntire
"Love Story" and "Betty" as sung by Taylor Swift
"Born to Run" as sung by Bruce Springsteen
"All Summer Long" as sung by Kid Rock
"America" by as sung by Simon & Garfunkel

SONGWRITING ACTIONS

Write a song like a movie—come up with a title, story plot, who's singing to whom—and then take out your camera and yell, "Action!"

Here are some "movie" song lyrics a few of my students have written:
One of my students was just starting her songwriting career when she wrote this gem. This song is so special to me because the movie within a lyric

she wrote was very specific in the socioeconomic world the characters lived in. It reminded me of a Fannie Flagg novel, like *Fried Green Tomatoes*.

Third Wheelin' at the Cracker Barrel
Lyrics by Hannah Marie Fasick (Used with Permission)

Verse 1
Leonard called it off again,
Said he wanted to be friends,
Called up my best girl Darlene,
She asked if there's anything I need.
Wanted to go to my favorite spot,
An old country store and restaurant,
She said she'd meet me there at eight,
And we could eat and commiserate.

Pre-chorus
Walked in, couldn't believe what I saw,
    Winkler: The scene at the restaurant starts
Darlene brought her boyfriend Paul.

Chorus
Now there ain't no worse feeling,
Than third wheeling,
At the Cracker Barrel,
At the Cracker Barrel,
I'm third wheeling,
At the Cracker Barrel.

Verse 2
I considered making a break for the door,
    Love all the specific furniture and tone in this verse
While we waited for a table, looked at home décor.
Distracted myself with the triangle peg game
They finally called out my damn name,
Leafing through the menu of homestyle cooking,

They were getting handsy, thought I wasn't looking.
My freshly broken heart was achin,'
So I ordered something with a shit ton of bacon

Pre-chorus
They snuck out to make out on a rocking chair,
> The plot thickens

I was hoping they got eaten by a black bear.

Chorus

Verse 3
Then out came our country fried steak,
> New scene—things only get worse for our heroine, while specific names for food come flying at us

Green beans, mac and cheese, nothing fake,
Side of biscuits, baked taters and dumplins.'
I never saw what happened next coming,
Before we even ordered dessert, I was in a whole new world of hurt.

Here is another "movie" song by my student Jamie Parsons that is chock-full of scenes that paint a picture and tell a story.

Franklin Road
Lyrics by Jamie Parsons (Used with Permission)

Verse #1
On a creaky back porch out in Tennessee,
> Winkler: Specific adjective and nouns

A candlelit table of fancy cheese,
An old wicker love seat off to the side,
Had some faded down pillows and an old cowhide.

Verse #2
Was a supermoon night with coyotes cryin,'
> Love "supermoon night" and the alliteration of coyotes cryin'

A solo cup full of cabernet wine,
   You can see and hear the next three lines
Country tunes mixed with '70s hits,
A little "Oh Black Betty Bam a Lam" for kicks.

Pre-chorus
The music turned slow,
   The scene begins and doesn't end until the last line of the chorus
I sipped my drink,
You pulled me off the wicker, whispered, "Dance with me."

Chorus
You spun me 'round and around and around and 'round,
You held me tight in the twinkle lights on a summer night,
Cheek to cheek,
Nose to nose,
You stole my heart,
On Franklin Road.

We fell in love on Franklin Road.

21
WRITING WITH COLLABORATORS

I've written with a lot of people—actually, hundreds. I consider myself musically promiscuous and I love it. And the only thing you can sometimes catch is a great song.

Here are some of the people I've worked with whose names you might recognize: Joe Sample, David Benoit, Freddie Hubbard, David Pomeranz, Dan Siegel, Michelle Brourman, Steve Tyrell, Dianne Reeves, and Lorraine Feather.

And there are many others that are fantastic and, perhaps, not so well known. Of course, I've written with jazz artists, but also country, R&B, and pop writers. Sometimes, the composer will take my lyric, go away and then present their music to my lyric. And sometimes they want me to be there while they're composing. There are those who like to write the music first, and then I like to go away and compose the lyrics. At times, we have a title and a good story concept, and we hash it out in the room together.

Each person has their little quirks and the way they do things. As the collaborators must respect that and actually jump on the bandwagon to make it work. You never know if the combination of you and the other person will work. I've written with people I've loved that have produced nothing and people who are diametrically opposed to me politically with whom I have created beautiful songs. You never know until the collaboration happens. Some writers are very methodical and detail-oriented, and some are seat-of-their-pants and unorganized, but brilliant. It seems a lot of them need deadlines to get the job done. And here's a little tip—always be nice to their spouse or significant other!

TOP 10 TIPS FOR COLLABORATORS

1. *Make their job easier:* Be prepared when you meet with a composer for a songwriting session. Share your titles folder, story plot ideas, and even full lyrics and lyric ideas that aren't entirely worked out yet. Involve your cowriter with your process and see which title, song, or idea fragment gets them most excited. Be sure to ask about the lyric ideas they have and listen to melodies on which they're working. It's a give-and-take process. When I go into a writing session, I have checked out my collaborator already. Songwriting is not a large world and it's fairly simple to ask around and get an accurate reading on a songwriter's character. You need to trust your cowriter.
2. *Be familiar with their work and comment on the things they do well:* Flattery will get you everywhere but do your research so you can be specific in your comments. I especially like mentioning songs of theirs that weren't hits or as well-known that are excellent. Remember, all their songs are their babies, not just the ones that are immediately recognized.
3. *Be versatile:* Be prepared to write a lyric to their melody or to have a whole lyric for them to which to put a melody. Also, be ready to sit in a room with them and work on the song together, with a guitar or piano right there, in real time.
4. *Be open:* There are many options when writing a song, and not just one way is the right way. When you collaborate with a partner, be ready to compromise and accept their idea if it's better.
5. *Agree on publishing terms before a song is written:* I always say that when I'm collaborating with someone, it's 50/50—we both own 50 percent of the song. If you think of the ownership of the song as a pie, 50 percent is *writer's share*, and 50 percent is *publishing*. The publishing share you can negotiate, if you bring a publisher on board (but be sure to have a legal agreement about what tangible things they will do for that percentage). I always say 50/50, no matter how much each partner contributes, because I believe doing this makes the process fairer. A percentage is not just based on what percentage of words or musical notes you wrote, but

that you showed up and are in partnership with your collaborator. For example, perhaps I only wrote 50 percent of the words but I came up with the title of the song and the story concept, and that's a lot! Always be generous when you are writing with a partner, if they're good they are worth that and a whole lot more.

Winkler digresses . . .
I was working on one of my musicals and it came time to write our collaborators' agreement, where the ownership percentages of the artistic parties are spelled out. I had been writing the musical with my two partners for about three years by then, and we had been through a lot with it: one well-received production, a lot of rebuffs from New York producers after a dizzying number of readings, but a very probable chance for a production at a prestigious theater. So, I was gobsmacked when one of my collaborators suddenly changed her mind on the 33.3 percent split among us three writers and instead wanted 42 percent based on a word count of the lyrics she'd written. It didn't work out for her; our very high-priced and experienced lawyer rolled his eyes and our other collaborator agreed. We each stayed at 33.3 percent.

6. *Be nice and enthusiastic:* If you're in a bad mood and you're grumpy, don't meet with your cowriter that day. This goes hand in hand with "make their job easier." Have a smile on your face, be enthusiastic, and don't bitch or spend your time gossiping and putting down your competitors. If I had a choice to write with a genius who made my writing life miserable or a very talented person who was a mensch (the Yiddish word for a good person), I'll pick the mensch every time.

7. *If you don't like something, say so:* I always think of writing with collaborators as a marriage, and to me, the marriage doesn't happen until the honeymoon is over. That means when you can honestly tell your collaborator you don't like their chorus, or the rhythm isn't working, or maybe that the melody just isn't cutting it for you. It does no good to hold it inside. Obviously, not everybody with whom I work takes criticism well, but everyone takes it in their own way. It's your job as an empathetic and supportive partner in rhyme to figure out how to do it. Some people like it unvarnished and straight; some like it with a little honey on top. It's

always smart to start with the things you like about the song. And some people are touchy and it's going to take them a little time to process it. I'm somewhat all three, depending on my mood.

8. *Always write with people on your level, and preferably better than you:* People who are better than you make you so much better. There are reasons they're better and if you keep your eyes open you can learn. And after all the years I've spent writing, I'm still learning. I'm always blown away by the sheer talent of the people with whom I work, which brings me to . . .

9. *Give your partner space to do their thing:* One of the great things about writing is finding a collaborator who will take your lyric that you thought was going to be a big Adele ballad and make it into a reggae song, and somehow it works! You're working with people for their input—so don't constrain them with too many rules. Don't be overly bossy and controlling (I'm speaking to myself here). Give your baby to the nice person over at the piano. They won't hurt it. And sometimes, they can make it into a miracle!

10. *Be a professional:* Be on time, plan for food breaks (songwriting makes me hungry—actually everything makes me hungry—but definitely songwriting), and have all the supplies you need to write. Little gifts are nice too. Collaboration is fun, big fun, so treat your cowriter really well. Because that person is going to write a hit with you, make you both a lot of money, and figure prominently in your autobiography.

I was trying to think of my best and worst writing experiences. I must say the best ones outnumber the bad ones by about 97 percent good to 3 percent bad. But it's always fun to talk about the train wrecks.

I was scheduled to write with a wunderkind keyboardist and arranger who was having quite a bit of success with this great pop/R&B hit on the radio. I was really excited to work with him, and he seemed nice when I'd talked to him on the phone. When I got to his apartment in the San Fernando Valley, I immediately noticed a weird smell coming from the shag carpets. But, at the door, he told me to take off my shoes to save the carpets (too late, buddy) and I did.

Evidently, he didn't believe in litter boxes for his three long-haired cats! One continually got up into my face and hissed and one shunned me while the third kept rubbing its body against my leg. From the minute I entered said residence, to the time I left, he wouldn't stop talking about all the records of his songs that were coming out. And when he stopped talking about the records, it was a gleeful retelling of musician gossip; always managing to put himself in the most favorable light. So finally, we got down to composing and he tells me he's picked a lyric from a couple that I had sent him, but he had to completely rewrite it. While he may have been a good melody writer, his talent did not extend to lyrics. When I told him that he'd lost my inner rhymes, he seemed unperturbed and, to be honest, uncaring. We finished the song, I put on my shoes, and bid him adieu. When I closed the door behind me, I breathed a sigh of relief to be rid of the whole stinky and, ultimately, brain-numbing experience, only to realize his cats had left me a little present in my shoe.

However, as a lyricist—the greatest gift has not been my royalties, but in the people with whom I work.

As a collaborator with great musicians and singers, I've gotten to hear Joe Sample and David Benoit play, had Dianne Reeves sing in my living room and witnessed grown people (called songwriters) so excited they seem like thirteen-year-olds! And with a cowriter, sometimes you witness that moment when the melody for a chorus appears, and you know you're going to be singing it for the rest of your life.

Phil Swann, who I have mentioned before as my cowriter on *Play It Cool*, is a real gas with whom to work. We met at the Songwriter's Guild of America when we were both teaching there. I guess it was fated we'd write together and be friends. We were both old hands at songwriting and we had both just had successful musicals playing in L.A. at the same time. He had a musical reworking of Romeo and Juliet called *The People vs. Friar Laurence* and I had *Too Old for the Chorus (But Not Too Old to be a Star!)*. Phil is from West Virginia, a country boy, by way of a few 1980s hair bands (a lot of spandex; I've seen the pictures). Phil plays good piano and sings well, so it is always fun working with him. We are well matched and our songwriting moves at the speed of light. We have no need to tell the other what needs to be done. Plus, when he isn't playing killer piano, he has a habit of pacing around with a tiny cigarillo in front of my house, until his next bolt of inspiration strikes. He is respectful, talented, eccentric, seasoned, and writes great songs.

Writing can be lonely and frustrating. Recently, I've taken to writing my lyrics with people. Through most of my career I'd do my lyrics alone, but I find with wonderful cowriters like Shelley Nyman, and Heather Perram Frank, I get more songs completed and have a better time doing it.

22
DIRTY LITTLE SECRETS OF SONGWRITING

For most of this book, I have guided you along on your songwriting journey in a gentle manner. When learning, I think everyone progresses better in a safe and nurturing environment. However, I think it's good to know some things about the songwriting life that I've learned along the way that aren't so nice and tidy. So here goes.

GOOD READER = GOOD WRITER

In my years of teaching songwriting, I can always tell when a songwriter is a reader—someone who can be found curled up with a book instead of binge watching or looking at their phone. The readers are always better writers. Why? The readers have had years of reading books by people who write professionally. In a way, they can mimic the different voices they've already heard in their minds. They consciously (or subconsciously) know what an adjective or verb is supposed to do. Their vocabulary is superior and, in general, they have ease with language that nonreaders don't have. Unfortunately, I wasn't there when you were seven years old to tell you this, but it's the truth. By the way, being a good speller doesn't seem to have anything to do with whether you are a good writer.

SHOW BUSINESS IS TOUGH

For many years, I dealt with publishers and record executives and temperamental singers. Then I got smart and carved myself a nice little world in which I can write and record. I have wonderful musicians with whom I work. I release my albums on my own label (nobody telling me what I should or should not do) and the critics and public like my work. But I'm a jazz singer/songwriter—that's a very small pond compared to wanting to be a pop performer or writer.

Everything is more complicated in pop music, where big money and superstardom are involved. The pressure that comes from that is intense. For some reason, a lot of people in the music business think it's perfectly okay to treat people badly. We all have been awakened by the #MeToo movement, but in my opinion, not enough attention has been drawn to the mental and sometimes physical abuse committed in the record business. It's not the ultra-encouraging world as portrayed by the judges of *American Idol* and *The Voice*. Rather, it can be an environment where the performer is sworn at, shamed, and made to feel diminished. I've had phones thrown at me, I've been screamed at on the phone for being "nothing more than a jazz singer," and generally treated like something usually found on the bottom of someone's shoe. We are dealing with reality here, and when you go out into the big world of show business, you're going to quickly notice this going on.

Recently, I invited a very successful record producer to come speak to my class. He had worked with some of the biggest stars of the last twenty years. I had met him at an industry luncheon and he was very charming, and I thought, "What the hell" and invited him to come speak to my class. He said he loved songwriters, especially ones just starting out. What could I lose? So, he came to my class, where he acted like he was auditioning everyone for a large record label, and generally treated my students like they were hopeless wannabes. When he left, I apologized to my students, and then one of them said something very wise: "Mr. Winkler, we know not everyone in the business is going to be as nice and encouraging as you, a lot of them will be like him." Therefore, piggybacking on that, if you want to be in the business, keep your eyes open—there are good people out there, find them and keep them in your circle. Be strong and don't take any shit. And if you get a chance to be part of the change, please take it.

TALENT ISN'T ENOUGH

After teaching now for nearly two decades, I've seen some wonderfully talented people pass through my classes. And occasionally, I've seen some people so talented that I've stepped forward to produce them. Even though these people had the whole package—great voice, great songs, good looks—I had to stop working with some of them. The reason was always the same—they didn't have the mental fortitude to take on the music business. This goes hand in hand with my last dirty little secret: the music business can be tough, unfair, frustrating, and insensitive. Successful people aren't just talented; they have amazing tenacity and resilience. They believe what they have is so incredible, nothing can stop them. And then they work for it 24/7.

I was lucky enough to work with, and be friends with, three-time GRAMMY-winning jazz vocalist Dianne Reeves. We met at the beginning of her career when she was first booked to play the prestigious Playboy Jazz Festival. At the time, she was playing a small café, the Comeback Inn in Venice, California, and had one album out on a small jazz label. I asked her if she was nervous and she shook her head no. Rather, she was sure she was going to wow the audience and recognized it as a great opportunity. Her attitude might have seemed a little too confident for some, except for the fact that her confidence passed the reality test. She does have one of the great voices in jazz and she did eventually wow the audience. Those are just the facts.

However, I've also worked with wonderful singers who aren't as confident, who shoot themselves in the foot and can't handle the many rejections and disappointments that are a daily part of show business. It's frustrating to see so much talent go unrecognized, but as I've noted, talent isn't enough.

IT TAKES TIME TO BE A CONSISTENT AND GOOD SONGWRITER

When young songwriters ask me how long it's going to take before they're going to be consistently good, I usually fudge the number and say six months to a year. The truth is that it's probably two years. I guess I hold off with telling them the truth, because in this TikTok world of short attention spans, that seems entirely too long and I don't want to scare anyone away. That's not saying in the two years you won't write good songs; it just means that your consistency will increase the longer you are at it. Songwriting is not easy, and learning the craft takes time.

IT'S ALWAYS PERSONAL

If the song doesn't resonate emotionally to you it won't resonate with anyone else. You've got to write songs that are full of emotion, that you feel very strongly about, and that you feel you can't wait to tell the world. Every time I hear "Shake It Off" by Taylor Swift, I know that at that moment in time, Taylor absolutely needed to write that song to shake off all the haters—it was part of her survival. There's a reason people say "Write what you know"; it's because only *you* will know the details of your story. And the songs don't have to be as emotionally fraught as Demi Lovato's "Dancing with the Devil." It can be fun like Meghan Trainor's "Dear Future Husband" or romantic as Kid Rock's "All Summer Long."

SAY WHAT ONLY YOU CAN SAY

This goes hand in hand with the last point. You all have a story, you've all lived a specific life, and you all have something to tell people that they wouldn't know if you didn't tell them. The individual details of your life only add specificity to the broader truths you're trying to communicate and won't limit the appeal of your song.

QUESTIONS ARE ALWAYS GOOD IN SONGS

Questions make you stop and think, they make the lyric sound more conversational, and they involve the audience even more in the song. When you hear a question, you want to answer it. It's just human nature. Some examples are "Is this the little girl I married?" from "Sunrise, Sunset," "Do Ya Think I'm Sexy?" by Rod Stewart or "Should I Stay or Should I Go?" by the Clash. There are a million of them.

OPPOSITES ARE GOOD IN SONGS

If you have a song with the word "day" in the title and it's professionally written, most likely "night" will be in the song somewhere too. Why? Because it reinforces the title and the story concept while giving some variety to the lyric. Some examples are "Late Night Talking" by Harry Styles where he says, "It's only been a couple of *days* and I miss you," or "A Hard Day's Night" by The Beatles, which has both opposites in the title.

IT'S ALWAYS WHO YOU KNOW

I've been in this business a long time, and I've never had anything good come from sending things cold. By that I mean just emailing a song, message, or CD to someone without a referral. That's a lot of nothing for a lot of years.

I got Liza Minnelli to sing my song (my first record cut) because I knew the producer. I was a waiter at a restaurant he frequented, and we had bonded over us both being young songwriters (see page 79 for the complete story).

My first record deal materialized because I had a connection to the small jazz label First American Records in Seattle. When I was a young man, I sold LPs at a swap meet, and Bill Metz, the general manager of the label, was a customer and we became friendly.

My first writing assignment for a musical came along because the guy picking the songs was my husband's best friend.

I got my first cut by number-one British jazz vocalist Claire Martin because her producer, Joel E. Siegel, knew me as a singer/songwriter, loved my album *Tales From Hollywood*, and told her to pick any song on it she wanted to sing.

Always look for a connection or an introduction to the producer or artist who you want to meet.

LEARNING IS NEVER A BAD THING

Sometimes, young songwriters don't want to learn an instrument or learn to read music or how to sing harmony because they feel too much education will somehow take the magic out of their songwriting.

But in my experience, playing an instrument or two or learning harmony will give songwriters more choices in creating their songs. It certainly has with me. The chordal patterns you go to differ when you're playing a piano or a guitar. When you play guitar, for most of us, your fingers go for the same comfortable chords. Switching to piano will immediately introduce your fingers to new voicings and different chord groupings.

For example, I think playing an instrument or a second instrument will give a songwriter more choices in creating their songs. The chordal patterns you go to will be different when you're playing a piano or a guitar. When you play guitar, for most of us, your fingers go for the same chords. Switching to piano will immediately introduce your fingers to new voicings and different chord groupings.

Additionally, knowing music theory can clearly tell you:

- What chord progressions work and what don't
- How to build your song so when the chorus comes—it pops
- How to create tension in your song and add more tonal variety
- Becoming skilled at singing harmony is great for creating new melodies. Why? Because each harmony line has its own melody.

SHAKE THINGS UP FROM TIME TO TIME

You can get stuck in a groove, into a habit, partial to what you've done before. The familiar can be very lulling and comforting. However, it's not always what's best for you as a songwriter. If you're writing a melody, switch instruments and maybe your fingers will fall into some new chordal voicings or sing your melody away from the piano—that's a really good thing to do. If your melody sounds good a cappella, it's only going to sound better with chords and other instruments. And from time to time, work with new co-writers, musicians, and producers. I find it's always fun and a little scary but ultimately rewarding to work with new people. You might just find someone who is the perfect combination to make your career really kick into third gear.

DON'T BELIEVE THE BEST THING SAID ABOUT YOU, DON'T BELIEVE THE WORST—THE TRUTH LIES IN THE MIDDLE

This next paragraph will prove one thing about me. I have cojones.

Here's the best review I've gotten in the last five years:

> "Mark Winkler is a musical marvel. Finally, a writer who sings, and a singer who can swing." —Rex Reed (a *New York Observer* writer who can be pretty scathing when he wants to be)

And here's the worst!

> In the two and half years I've been doing concert reviews, I've seen literally hundreds of shows—and without a doubt, some of the best ones have been Jazz Live presentations at the Saville Theatre. Sadly, last night's performance by Mark Winkler was not one of them. . . . I had conflicting clues about the gig. On one hand, some glowing reviews of Winkler CDs from the likes of allaboutjazz.com

and *Jazz Times*. On the flip side, a friend with serious jazz listener credentials warned that, "... his vocals sound like fingernails on a blackboard to me."
—Robert Bush, *San Diego Reader*

The truth, as it often does, is probably somewhere in between those extremes. I'm probably not a musical marvel, but I'm probably not Yoko Ono either!

Some artists never read their reviews; I usually do. But the reality test is the general consensus of the reviews that you are getting. And most importantly, are you booking gigs and putting out albums? If everywhere you turn the bad reviews are creeping in, you can't get booked and no one wants to record you, those are the things you should be looking at. And truthfully, reviews can point out things that are working and things that aren't.

DON'T BE CHASING THE LATEST BIG TREND

When I was a young songwriter, the publishers I went to were always chasing after yesterday's biggest hit. They literally wanted a facsimile of whatever was topping the charts. Guess what? Yesterday's biggest hit is gone before tomorrow comes. Of course, there are some things in the musical landscape that I think will be around for a while—rap and hip-hop's pervasive rhythms have been transplanted to everything from Ed Sheeran songs to Florida Georgia Line country bro numbers. Also, the use of synthesizers isn't going anywhere. However, a lot of sounds, vocal affectations, and unusual instruments will come and go. Follow your own muse and write the song that can be the next big trend.

DON'T BE AGE-INAPPROPRIATE

Pop, country, R&B, and hip-hop are the most visible and probably lucrative markets for a songwriter. And these genres are bought, downloaded, and sampled by a very young demographic. That's just reality. The people who write the hit songs or cowrite with the young talent are generally no more than ten to fifteen years older. Which means that when you are a forty or forty-five-year-old songwriter, you're getting to be in the minority. I believe it's a little older in country and probably younger in hip-hop and rap. Always write about subjects that reflect who you are now. Don't be writing about puppy love and high school romances if it's been decades since you've experienced them. It's not suddenly going to make you look commercial, but it will suddenly make you look foolish.

Winkler digresses . . .
About fifteen years ago, I was teaching at the Songwriters Guild when this lovely lady, Christel Alexander, probably in her sixties, presented me with a song to hear. I asked her who it was for, and she said Britney Spears, who at that time was still a few years away from snakes and closer to schoolgirl uniforms. As expected, the song's lyrics had about as much relevance to Britney as a Cole Porter patter song. I asked her about herself, and she opened up to me about her fascinating life growing up as a little girl in Germany during World War II, losing her father, hiding out with her grandparents and almost starving. I found it so fascinating, I worked with her on developing those songs for a one-woman show called My Berlin, *which she has now done many times to much success in cabaret venues. Musical theater, jazz, cabaret, and gospel are ageless genres and worthy avenues to pursue.*

And here's the good news. As our population is getting older, it seems more opportunities are being created for individuals of a certain age. Cher had number-one hits with "Believe" when she was over fifty and "DJ Play a Christmas Song" when she was over seventy. Bruce Springsteen had a successful one-man show featuring his music on Broadway, and Cyndi Lauper had a Tony Award–winning musical *Kinky Boots* as she approached her sixties. Maybe you'll be a trailblazer too.

THERE ARE FRIENDS . . . AND THEN THERE ARE BUSINESS ASSOCIATES
Show business is a funny business because it puts you in contact with fellow songwriters and musicians in physically close situations where you bear your darkest secrets and (musically at least) put it out on the line. You get to meet your cohort's significant others, kids, dogs, and sometimes, after a rehearsal or writing session, share some deep conversation. But that doesn't mean they're your friends. It means they're a business associate you really like. And that's a difference that's good to know. Early in my career, I kept getting hurt because my "friends" weren't calling me up to go out to eat or see a movie or

do, you know, "friend" things. That's when my very wise husband imparted this wisdom to me, and I've never forgotten it.

SOMETIMES THE NICEST PEOPLE AREN'T VERY TALENTED

Wouldn't it be great if your nicest friend was the most talented person on the planet, and you could just work with them and write and write and write? Guess what folks! Usually, your best friend is just that—your best friend. And when you are working with songwriters and musicians you need the "best" people you can find—and sometimes they're not the nicest people.

There's a litany of famous people, and we all love their music, but when you read their biographies you find yourself thinking, "Wow, how could that schmuck write such sensitive and beautiful material?"

I had a favorite male singer, with a voice like a choirboy, who decided to record one of my songs. I pinched myself at my good fortune, until I went to the recording session. He was one of the most disagreeable and nasty people I had ever met. After a glorious vocal take, I gave him a compliment and he responded like I had just told him he was awful. Yes, he was a recovering addict and was a little down on his luck at the time, but the guy had a total break with reality. However, he sang beautifully!

So, your mission is to find wonderfully talented people to work with who are "nice" and "respectful" with great work habits. It can be done because I've done it. Don't put up with lovely people who are honestly not that good, but don't put up with great musicians who are prima donnas either.

REHEARSE THE MAGIC

Anybody who knows me knows I like to rehearse. First of all, I love to sing with great musicians and (if I'm not on the road all the time) when I'm putting a show together, I need the rehearsal to work out elements in the charts and with my vocals that I would normally woodshed on tour. Only the process of playing in a room with real musicians will give you that experience. I like to try different things with a song, even if it already has a solid arrangement, and leave it open for my wonderful and knowledgeable musicians to make what is good even better.

I was doing a gig a few years ago with a musician who assured me we had two hours to rehearse our fifty-minute show (ten songs) and then decided after we went through the tunes quickly that he wanted the rehearsal to end. He said, "Let's not spoil the magic." I looked at him, reminded him of his two-hour promise and said, "Let's *rehearse* the magic!"

ALWAYS ASK TO HEAR AN MP3 OR MP4 OR SOME OF THEIR SONGS ON A STREAMING SERVICE BEFORE YOU WRITE WITH SOMEONE

In the analogue universe, sometimes I'd meet a very nice songwriter and they'd want to write with me, and I'd say, "Come on over to my place and I can hear some of your songs." I wasted many an afternoon listening to bad songs all the way through and then sometimes having lunch with the always nice but most always not-so-talented songwriter.

Winkler digresses . . .

Confession time—I hate hearing bad songs. And a lot of the time I find them funny, which is not a very nice thing to say. I spent some time with a friend of a friend at a party and he told me he was a songwriter. He seemed smart and I thought "What the hell, I'll invite him over." He put on his cassette tape (this was some time before the internet) and out came the most disjointed mumbo-jumbo of a laundry list song I had ever heard. I believe he was comparing his love to the things he loved like, "Eartha Kitt, puppy dog bottoms, seltzer water and the Grand Coulee Dam." I had to train my drishti on the light fixture above his head not to completely collapse in laughter. It was very difficult.

To conserve your time, ask for a link to their best songs—short and sweet. You'll thank me for the rest of your life.

BE NICE TO THE SPOUSES AND SIGNIFICANT OTHERS OF THE PEOPLE YOU WORK WITH

Musicians are always working and thinking about music, so, in a lot of situations, it's up to their spouses or partners to take care of things like opening the door for you, scheduling appointments, and making you a nice cup of coffee. Hats off to them, because, in addition to their own jobs and everyday duties, they usually run the life of their "little geniuses." A great tip to know is you can never lose by making them your friend. Because of course, they always weigh in on the writing partners their husband or wife is working with. Spouses love me because I'm polite, sincere with compliments, and actually treat them like a person. Which, when you think about it, is only right.

ALWAYS SHARE YOUR GLORY WITH OTHERS
It's no surprise that a lot of people in the music business are egocentric, but the truth about the music business is that it's not done alone. Rather, as a songwriter or performer you are often only as good as the people surrounding you. So, when good things happen to you, be sure to thank the people who helped you via your social media and in your live shows. A little generosity of spirit goes a long way.

SOME PEOPLE WILL RESENT YOUR SUCCESS
Show business is a tough, tough field to go into and let's face it, a lot of people pursuing it won't make it. One of the saddest things I've learned is that people actually can turn on you if you've had a little success. Suddenly as a peer, you are a threat to where they fit in this music world you share. Stick with the colleagues who are in your corner through thick and thin and let the others fall away.

KEEP LISTENING TO CURRENT MUSIC
Music is always changing. While the basic structures of songwriting have remained relatively stable through the years, things such as instrumentation, rhythms (beats), vocal techniques, and vernacular used in songs are always updating. It wasn't too long ago when banjos and whistling and even trumpet solos were happening. The only way to keep up with this is to keep up with current music on streaming and radio outlets. This goes for all genres of music. Nothing is as bad as someone whose music is stuck in the early aughts or 1995.

ONE PLUS ONE DOESN'T EQUAL TWO
Here are two dirty little secrets in one: music is magical, and one plus one doesn't always equal two. When you enter into a collaboration, the product you come up with is always different than what you would have done alone. Most of the time it's primarily what you'd expect; at times the two of you write badly together, then sometimes, KAZOOOWIE!!—it's mystical, mysterious,

and wonderful, just like eating fried chicken on a Sunday morning" (that's what my pal and musical engineer Nolan Shaheed says after a particularly good take). It's happened to me quite a few times in my writing career, and it's something I never take for granted or can figure out—because it's alchemy—and I only want to keep the relationship going with the partner whose combination with me is so wonderful.

IT'S ULTIMATELY WHAT YOU SAY THAT MATTERS

I can teach anyone the basic techniques to writing songs. They are well-established—all it takes is a little discipline and practice and time. However, not everyone has something to say—and it's what you say that matters.

More often than not, some people are afraid to express the emotion inherent in something that's personal and unique to them. Other people have a good relationship with their emotional life and feel fairly comfortable turning on the faucet and filling their songs with their deepest and darkest secrets. Most of us are between the two, navigating the dance between how much we'll reveal, and won't. It's the bravery of the reveal that can really make your song so special. It's the stories, the particular point of view, and the thought that feels new and unsaid that makes songwriting truly special.

23

AM I DOING THIS THING RIGHT?

Here's a checklist of *techniques* that you need when writing lyrics. You may see some repetition from other places in the book, but repetition is a good thing in songwriting and in learning our craft.

Definition of "Technique"
- The manner with which a musician uses the specific technical skills of a chosen field of music.
- A skill in a particular field.

Each genre of music may require one or more techniques. When writing in a particular musical style, it's your job to listen to enough of the best songs in that genre to know the rules. Clever rhyming is highly valued in musical theater, hip-hop, and cabaret but not so much in pop or rock. Furniture is highly valued in country, pop, and musical theater but not so much in EDM or in some urban music. Generally, you should be able to check off about 80 percent of the genre-specific elements or components on this list to be sure that your song is working. And to answer your next question: Yes, it's as easy—and as hard—as that.

- *Come up with a great title.* Then "write to title" by creating a compelling story plot for that title. It's always effective to say the familiar in an unfamiliar way.

- *Be specific.* Remember that the specificity you use in a song is the portal into a greater universal emotion or truth. Your song must resonate with people. We are living in a very polarized and fragmented society. So, study the audience for whom you're writing and proceed accordingly. Even better, understand your unique community and write specifically for your "tribe."
- *Be authentic.* Nobody likes a liar in this society. All great songs are from the heart and that's why they resonate with the listener. If you don't truly feel it, nobody else will either.
- *Touch somebody.* Songs are emotional, not cerebral creatures. After a successful show, people don't come up to me and discuss my inner rhymes or alliterative techniques. They come up to me with tears in their eyes and tell me how a song has touched them or made them smile or maybe tap their feet.

Winkler digresses . . .

"Scattin' in the Moonlight," a song on my first album, got a lot of airplay on jazz and "Quiet Storm" radio stations. One day, I got a letter from a woman from Orlando, Florida. Her husband had recently undergone emergency heart surgery and asked that the song be played during the procedure, because it reminded him of his wife and the way she would unconsciously sing to herself when she thought no one was listening (the plot of my song). He recovered from the surgery and she just wanted to thank me for getting her husband through this terrible ordeal. To me that's what it's all about. Touching people.

- *Know your form, inside and out.* My biggest surprise as a songwriting teacher is the correlation between a deep understanding of form and the eventual quality of a song.
- *Not all lines in a song are of equal importance.* The first line of the verse, the last line of the verse (or pre-chorus), and the first and last line of the chorus are the most important lines in a verse/chorus song. Don't save your best lines for the second line of the second verse.
- *Use a variety of rhymes in a song.* Your facility with rhyming sometimes has a direct correlation with how clever and talented people think you are (Stephen Sondheim, anyone?). Masculine, feminine, three- and four-rhymes, and perfect and imperfect rhyming are all great to do and lend variety to your songs. A little note: the more unusual your rhyming words, the better

the rhyme. "Day" and "way" aren't so thrilling, but "crustacean" and "train station" are quite skillful. Inner rhymes are great to use too—that's rhyming a word in the middle of a line with a word at the end of the line: "Mere *alcohol* doesn't thrill me at *all*" in Cole Porter's, "I Get a Kick Out of You." Inner rhyming speeds up a lengthy line.

- *Always be conversational in your songs.* Use the natural rhythm of conversational speech; each word's syllables must be stressed naturally. Sometimes, you may try to be too fancy or profound or poetic in a song, when all that's needed is a conversational and concise way of reaching the listener, much like talking to a friend. Often, I speak my lyrics out loud to make sure they ring true.
- *Tell a story.* You should always be able to answer these three questions:
  - Who's singing?
  - To whom are they singing?
  - What are they trying to accomplish in the song?

    The tone of the song is important. You do not have to specify the location or time of day in the lyrics, but it's important that you know the where and when of your tale. For example, the tone you would use in bed while talking to your lover is very different than talking to your brother in the kitchen.
- *The music and the lyric must fit together to achieve prosody.* The lyrics should fit the scansion (the rhythm) of the line. Generally, nouns and verbs are on longer-held notes than conjunctions (but, and, so). No stretching out words (I dislike putting the word "and" on two notes) and no cramming in words either. One syllable to one note. Single syllable words get one note; they need to flow naturally. And think about the melody line; don't put the word "down" on the highest note in a phrase.
- *A picture tells a thousand words.* "Picture words" or "furniture" (specific versus generic nouns and verbs) are wonderful things to have in songs. I've rarely seen an instance where drawing a picture or setting a scene or making the verse into a little movie didn't work in a song. It immediately makes things specific and the lyrics "show" instead of "tell."
- *Repetition is a good thing.* Hooks, certain lines, and musical phrases are wonderful things to repeat in a song. New songwriters use far too little repetition in their songs. There is a need to have sections in a song that feel familiar to the listener and repetition is an excellent way of accomplishing that.

- *Alliteration enhances songs.* For example, "sweet, summer sensation."
- *"Show, don't tell" is a wonderful writing technique.* It works perfectly with specificity and picture words. "You left me and broke my heart" isn't nearly as captivating as "I caught you sneaking out with your suitcase and plane tickets for two, and when the door slammed, I cried myself to sleep and pretended I never loved you."
- *Anaphora can be powerful in songs.* That's starting the first part of each line in a verse or chorus with the same three or four words. For example, "I wish you this . . . I wish you that" or "I hope this . . . I hope that." Anaphora can be used in any section of the tune, and goes naturally with . . .
- *Laundry list songs are a songwriter's best friends.* The very form of "laundry list songs" compels the songwriter to use pictures and repetition and anaphora, which is a reasonably good way to start writing a song.
- *Each section of a tune must be easily identifiable.* Your chorus shouldn't be indistinguishable from your verse, your bridge from your chorus. They should each have their own scansion, rhyme words, and place in the overall scale of the key you are in. Generally, the chorus is higher than the verse melodically, and the bridge climbs up to the chorus note wise.
- *Your song can't depend on footnotes or explanations (obviously).* It must stand on its own. In my classes, and I'm sure in songwriting classes and publisher's offices everywhere, writers frequently introduce songs with a "disclaimer." While I often find it charming, and sometimes important for me as a teacher, in the actual finished song, it's unnecessary.
- *Your song must portray the singer/narrator in a good light.* Perhaps in rap and musical theater they can be bad guys, but in all other genres they're the heroes and heroines.
- *Your songs must have a good beat.* Use a fun groove or rhythmic component that makes people want to move. Most hit songs are up-tempo or mid-tempo. That's not to say a variety of rhythms don't make it in popular music—Adele brought ballads back in a big way. I'm just saying that most hit songs are mid- or up-tempo.
- *Your songs must complement the vocal range and personality of the singer who sings it, stressing all their strengths and minimizing their shortcomings.* For Ariana Grande and Kelly Clarkson, a lot of high notes and wide range; for Miranda Lambert or Tim McGraw—more conversational and a story with an attitude.

To conclude: being a songwriter is being able to balance all these techniques, and say something with an arresting point of view, all atop a melody that is catchy and hummable at the same time. When all the balls are in the air and the trick is working—it's quite the magic.

24

YOU CAN WRITE A SONG

Wanna know a little secret? If you have your *craft* down, you can write a song just about any time you want to: no writer's blocks or wandering around in the desert looking for clues. Sometimes it's more romantic to say writing the song was a "journey" or took weeks or came to you in a dream or a moment of divine inspiration. However, I'm more the divine perspiration type. And special note, I know writers are people and some songwriters have all sorts of triggers.

As noted before, I've known many accomplished musicians who would wait until the very last minute and then write a brilliant song, but they needed the timeclock to get them there. To me, one of the great joys of writing songs consistently over a long period of time is that I can write them relatively effortlessly, relatively fast. And I think you can too. There is alchemy in songwriting and I'm not saying every time you write something on assignment it's going to be fantastic, but it will be professional and if you have a commission or assignment deadline, you will meet it.

When faced with an assignment, use these techniques and formulas to write the lyric. If you follow them, the song will be written:
- Come up with the title of the song. Make sure it's a good one.
- Come up with a story plot that fits the title (write to title).
- Who's singing? Who are they singing to?
- What are they trying to accomplish?

- What's your form (verse/chorus or AABA)?
- Now, tell the story as if you're conversing with a friend.
- On the first go round, don't worry about all the lines being good.
- Use a variety of rhymes in the song.
- Use "furniture" in the song.
- Make sure the song has an emotional resonance to you.
- Make sure there's some lyrical repetition in the song (definitely the hook).
- Use anaphora or alliteration in the song when possible.

When you're starting out as a songwriter, there are holes in your knowledge that may serve as stumbling blocks. However, if plan A isn't working, when you're a pro, you can go to plan B or C because you have the tools in your toolbelt to do the job.

If the song isn't working, perhaps your concept isn't strong enough. If your title and story/concept are rock-solid, you'll have a much easier go with it.

For instance, you may need more "furniture" in the song. Or there are too many clichés in the lines or not enough repetition. Also, make sure you know what each section of the tune must accomplish. *The verses are for story and the chorus is for stating the theme of the song and drawing in the listener with repetition and a good hook.*

A few years ago I was working on a David Benoit album. David is a wonderful pianist who has had many smooth jazz and mainstream jazz hits over the years with his covers of Vince Guaraldi's Charlie Brown songs and his own highly melodic originals. Finally, he was going to be doing an album of his original songs with some of his favorite lyricists, myself included. He gave me two melodies to work on, plus the third song on the album would be a tune we'd already written from an unproduced musical from several years prior, about the last months of Marilyn Monroe's life called *Something's Got to Give*.

While he was showing me the songs he had written for the new project, there was one tune in particular that jumped out at me. It was a rhythmic, almost Bacharach-like tune. When I expressed my passion for the song, he said he'd already promised Brenda Russell that she'd be writing the lyrics for it (Brenda Russell has written countless hit songs like "Get Here," "Piano in the Dark," and the musical *The Color Purple*). I liked the melody so much, I asked David if I could have an MP3 of it. For the next week, I played it in my car incessantly. I just loved it.

Mark (left) with David Benoit recording his album 2 In Love (photo by Richard Del Belso).

About six days before the session, I got a call from David saying Brenda Russell was in the middle of another assignment that wasn't done and couldn't write the lyric. Faster than you can say "I know I can write it!" I said I'd have it done in six days. I knew I could do it in two, but I always give myself the longest period I can to write for projects. Because if you tell them you can do something in two days, next time they'll want it in one day.

The next day I found myself at the funeral of a business associate of my husband, his former boss at Warner Bros., Sandy Reisenbach, and sometime in the middle of the rabbi's speech about "life being a dance that Sandy never failed to dance," the lyric started writing itself. And the good news was a lot of my work was done.

From playing it over and over, I'd learned the melody and knew the form of the song and where to place the title. And the rabbi's sermon gave me my story plot and even led to my title.

I went home after the service and wrote "This Dance" and then waited four more days to give it to David. You can find it on his wonderful recording, *2 In Love*.

"This Dance"
Lyrics by Mark Winkler

Verse #1
Life's very short
And no one can hold back time.
So, don't put off your dreams,
Thinking your dreams will be fine.

Chorus
Go for the best,
Damn all the rest.
We only get one chance,
Go on, do things your way.
We've just got today;
We only get this dance.

Verse #2
Don't be afraid
Before the band has played.
Listen with your heart
And play the song you long to hear.

Chorus
Go for what's new,
Shake it up too
Don't tell 'em in advance.
Darling, once round the floor,
Leave them wanting more,
We only get this dance.
Make it bold,
Take a chance,
I've been told,
We only get this dance.

Mark (left) with Steve Tyrell and his producer Barbara Brighton while recording their duet of "But It Still Ain't So" (photo by Richard Del Beso).

Winkler digresses . . .

In 2016, I did an album called The Company I Keep *on which I collaborated with different artists. On this record, I was very pleased to be working with a singer that I admire greatly—Steve Tyrell. Steve has worn many hats in the music business; he has been a movie studio executive, a gold record–awarded songwriter and producer, and a singing star. He'd come to see one of my shows a few years previously and as a DJ on L.A.'s jazz station, KJZZ, he'd been playing my songs, so I knew he was a fan. When the collaboration project happened, I jumped at asking him to be on it and he said yes.*

Eight years ago, Trump was running for president, and my little song was about a lyin' and cheatin' politician. Ironically, it did bear more than a passing resemblance to him, so what could be more perfect? To be sure, I asked Steve if he felt comfortable singing the song with this lyrical content and he said he'd sing "anything" I wanted.

The day of the session was a dream. First of all, we did the vocals in his home studio with his engineer who was on top of it all. And Steve turned out to be the hardest working singer I'd ever worked with—he literally would not stop until his part was perfect. As good as he was as a singer, that's how good he was at knowing what the song needed vocally from both of us.

The song is AABA, which is the form used by most writers during the Great American Songbook era. AABA is still the one used most by jazz singers today.

Here's the lyric:

"But It Still Ain't So" (Duet)
Lyrics by Mark Winkler

First A: Mark Winkler

You can say that the world is flat,
That a leopard's pure pussycat.
You can talk trash
Like you really know,
Gimme hard cash—but it still ain't so.

Second A: Steve Tyrell

You can brag that a shark won't bite
And inform me your wrong is right.
You can dress up
Put on quite a show
Even fess up—*Mark*: But it still ain't so.

I was rehearsing with my band when I got a fateful call from Steve. By the time we'd recorded the song, Trump had won the election and the country was divided very bitterly down the middle. Steve had just gotten off the phone with his manager who wasn't happy about our little duet. Steve said he'd record anything else I wanted him to but releasing our duet "But It Still Ain't So" was a "no." I told Steve I'd think about it and get back to him when I left the rehearsal, and we could talk more.

This is when "experience" is a godsend. I knew "But It Still Ain't So" was a laundry list song, and the great thing about them is you can replace one list for another—you get where I'm going. I made the cheatin' and lyin' politician I was talking to into a cheatin' and lyin' woman. And before you could say, "I can write it!" it was written on the back of a magazine in forty-five minutes in my car going home from the rehearsal. Keep in mind that many years of experience went into the feat, and, yes, I'm proud of it.

I read Steve the new lyric. He couldn't believe I'd written it so fast. In a couple of days we recorded the song that you can find on my recording, *The Company I Keep*. Here are the lyrics:

But It Still Ain't So
Lyrics by Mark Winkler

First A: Mark

You can say that I rock your world
When I kiss you, your toes all curl.
You can talk trash, put on quite a show,
Whisper sweet things, but it still ain't so.

Second A: Steve
Ooh you can feed me a T-bone steak,
Lots of gravy and chocolate cake.
You can dress up in something nice and low,
C'mon baby serve me, but it still ain't so.

I've learned after many years that when writing a song, there are many ways you can do it. And in songwriting as well as in life, having options is a lovely thing.

Here's a lyric to an old song I wrote a few years ago. I got the title from a James Ellroy book I love called *The Big Nowhere*.

"The Big Nowhere" (Version One)
Lyrics by Mark Winkler

Verse #1:
It's kinda Zen, it's kinda kooky
It's definitely not what they teach you
In the movies

Verse #2:
It's laid out flat, you could get lost there
They say it's just an offramp to paradise
But they don't tell you the cost dear.

Chorus:
They call this city "The Big Nowhere,"
It's got no center anywhere.
But still the dreamers come in quite unprepared
To get their share of "The Big Nowhere."
Beware! of "The Big Nowhere"!

I wrote this lyric quickly, and what you're seeing is probably a second draft. The first rule I broke was that the scansion between the verses doesn't match. But there were lines I liked in the song. The first line "It's kinda Zen, it's kinda kooky" is a grabber and "just an offramp to paradise" is a good line. And there are some nice double rhymes—"lost there" and "cost dear"—however, overall, it left me feeling flat. It has a breezy, yet whimsical tone in describing my fair city Los Angeles.

But there's really no involvement on my part; I'm just blithely throwing out thoughts on the city to a universal you. What I am trying to do is be clever. Not good enough. So, after a week, I went back to the drawing board and wrote a second "much better" song that can be found on my album *Tales from Hollywood*.

In the second version, I'm a detective investigating a murder of a beautiful girl in Hollywood for whom I have some feelings. It's basically a James Ellroy or Raymond Chandler forties mystery novel in four minutes—with a beginning, middle, and end! I'm not just whimsically talking about Los Angeles, I'm a hard-boiled, yet slightly weary detective living out a story in Los Angeles. Here's what it's got:

- Good title
- Good story written to title
- The stakes are high (I care for the girl); the villain is bad and I solve the case
- Tight structure—every verse advances the story
- It plays like a movie with plenty of "furniture" that references an earlier time period and is true to the detective genre like "Hudson" and "all night stake-out"
- It has a cynical, yet playful tone
- Good hook: "Beware! Beware! Beware in this city they call the 'Big Nowhere'"—which is the only thing I took from the prior song (alliteration always works)

"The Big Nowhere" (Version Two)
Lyrics by Mark Winkler

Verse #1:
Fingerprints on broken glass,
A trail of clues goin' nowhere fast,
I'm in a cheap crash pad just off of Vine,
All night stakeout on overtime.

Verse #2:
When this monster Hudson rounds the curve,
Streets are slick—the Hudson swerves,
I grab some coffee to calm my nerves,
Wearin' my shades at night 'cause the moonlight hurts.

Chorus:
Steady boy, hey what's the deal?
Has this case got you out in left field?
In dreamsville with some angel eyes,
Stop you're dreamin' she's cold as ice.
Beware! Beware! Beware! Baby beware
In this city they call "The Big Nowhere!"

SONGWRITING ACTIONS

Find an old song of yours that doesn't quite work and rewrite it. You can use the existing lyrics from the old song and update them with the knowledge you have now or keep only the title and story/concept and write a whole new song. It's up to you.

25
A SONG IS LIKE A HOUSE

Writing a song has a lot in common with constructing a high-quality house. Perhaps I've been watching too many episodes of *The Property Brothers*, but just like a house, a song must have "good bones."

So, here's a good visualization checklist for constructing your songs:

1. *Foundation:* The song has a solid story plot that can be told in two sentences.
2. *Walls:* You can identify easily who is singing, who they're singing to, what they are trying to accomplish in the song, and that the tone of song is consistent.
3. *Roof:* The song has hooks, is catchy, and memorable. It has repeated lyrical sections and a good "payoff" line in the chorus.
4. *Furniture:* It has specific nouns and verbs that are "picture words."
5. *Front door:* It has a universal and relatable emotion that welcomes the listener into the song.
6. *Floor plan:* The song adheres to the song form you've chosen, with each section flowing well into the next. Each section of the song accomplishes its mission (you don't want your bedroom being used as a bathroom!).
7. *Rooms:* Each one-rhyme (masculine rhyme) is a half of a room. Each two-rhyme (feminine rhyme) and three-rhyme is one room. The more rooms, the better.

8. *Windows:* The lyric is clear and conversational. It progresses in a logical and natural way.
9. *Custom touches:* A lot of similes, metaphors, alliteration, anaphora, and vocables.
10. *Curb appeal:* A good title and appealing subject matter.
11. *Location:* The song is true to its (marketable, viable, or ascribed) genre, and fulfills all the rules of the genre.

SONGWRITING ACTIONS

Now, strap on your toolbelt and build a house (song). Take a familiar song, or a song that you've written, and see how much of the house you've built. Once you've checked off all the requirements, it may be time to sell and get top dollar.

26
PUBLISHING AND COPYRIGHTING

For some reason, the concept of publishing always gets my students buzzing. I mention the word and the next hour is spent talking and debating about it. I sometimes find that the topic is baffling to my students, but let me try to explain it in a clear, and hopefully digestible, way.

Most newbie songwriters have heard the adage that publishing is really the cornerstone of wealth in the music business. That axiom is true—the published song's earnings are the gift that keeps on giving. If you write a hit song, the initial earnings will probably be considerable, though not as considerable now in the age of streaming. However, if the song has the potential for a life after its initial chart run, such as placements in movies, TV shows, commercials, and subsequent recordings by other artists, the resulting monies can be significant. Mariah Carey and Whitney Houston were both gigantic superstars in the nineties, but in terms of actual wealth, Mariah Carey earned far more because she wrote or cowrote almost all her hit songs.

In the old days of the music business, songwriters were routinely pressured into giving away their share of publishing. This was disproportionately true for Black songwriters. And in the not-so-distant past, superstar singers would magically have their names appear in the credits on songs they didn't write. Elvis Presley didn't write songs, but his manager, Colonel Parker, made sure his name was on many of his songs, and the quality of the songs he recorded (especially the ones he sang in the movies) precipitously went down when the

Colonel demanded that the songwriters give him the publishing for the songs. The great songwriting team of Leiber and Stoller, who wrote many of Elvis's early songs (like "Jailhouse Rock") wouldn't accept the deal and stopped writing for him.

More recently, due to the increased awareness of this practice and the litigious nature of the music business, managers and lawyers aren't successful in putting their superstar's name on songs anymore. Diane Warren, who is inarguably one of the most successful commercial songwriters ever, formed her own publishing company, Realsongs, early in her career and is the sole writer for a large percentage of her songs. According to various media, her song catalogue is worth upward of $150 million and the only artist catalogues that are bigger monetarily are The Beatles' and Michael Jackson's.

Think of the publishing—the ownership of the song—as a pie, and the whole pie represents 100 percent.

Fifty percent of the pie is the writer's royalties and 50 percent of it is the publisher's royalties. One thing to remember is that a writer or writers can give away any proportion of the publishing they want, but no one can legally take a writing credit away.

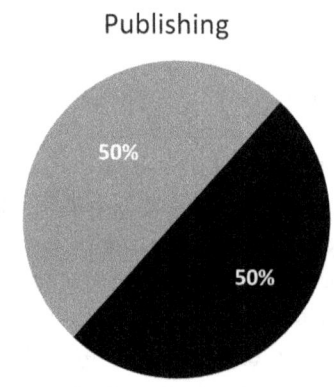

What I tell songwriters to do is very straightforward: before you start cowriting any songs, schedule a time to talk about the percentage each songwriter is taking. Don't be uneasy and postpone it until you and your co-writer(s) have a song, or until the demo is recorded and definitely not after the song is recorded.

Winkler digresses . . .

In my early songwriting days, I cowrote a single for a well-established R&B singer. I wrote it with a well-connected songwriter who'd had many more cuts than I had. I didn't see or sign my publishing agreement with him until after the record was cut and scheduled to come out. When I got the agreement, which his lawyer had drawn up, I had 33 percent of the writers' credit and none of the publishing. The single was midcharting and I missed out on quite a lot of income. He promised me many more cuts to come and I, being young and leery of a confrontation, didn't press the point.

Here's the proper thing to do: *before you write a note of the song, work out with the other writers how you want to split the pie.* Generally, if I'm working with one other writer, I like to do a 50/50 split.

Perhaps you're working with a melody writer that contributes a couple of lines or even a verse to a song lyrically as well. You might think they should get 60 percent or 65 percent, but the truth is it's not the amount of words or notes each party writes in a song, but the fact that each party is in a room (or Zooming or on the phone) and bouncing ideas off each other and creating the song *together*. It's that alchemy that makes the song. Often, the people you're writing with are not your friends—they're "business associates." And it sometimes may be intimidating to talk business immediately in a situation with someone you don't know but do it in a friendly and businesslike way. You'll be glad you did.

An exception to this is when someone hires you as the songwriter to write a song for a flat fee. That's called "work for hire." The company or employer under copyright law is then considered the legal author. You are paid a set fee for your writing and do not share in any royalties or further income coming from the song. Occasionally, I've been hired to write a song for a specific commercial or a bit of special material for a performer with the stipulation that the product in the commercial or the performer owns the song. I only do this when I feel certain that the song would have no afterlife.

Winkler digresses again . . .

I love the singer/songwriter Bobby Troup. He's written or cowritten such fantastic songs as "Baby, Baby All the Time," "Daddy," "Girl Talk," "The Meaning of the Blues," and "(Get Your Kicks on) Route 66," which has been covered by everyone from Nat King Cole to Depeche Mode to the Rolling Stones. It's truly a standard.

The song came about when Bobby was traveling from Pennsylvania to Los Angeles in a brand-new convertible with his first wife, Cynthia, to meet with Nat King Cole. He planned to pitch "Baby, Baby All the Time," but needed another song to show Nat. While driving along Route 66, he got the idea to write a jivey blues song about his road trip just perfect for the Cole trio. Somewhere on the road Cynthia whispered this lyric in his ear: "Get your kicks on Route 66." It's the hook of the whole song. Bobby usually wrote alone and Cynthia's name doesn't appear on the song. It was a different time; she was his wife, and she didn't have a good lawyer. I've done two albums of his tunes and have gotten to know his wonderful family who says that Bobby recognized the part Cynthia played in the creation of his biggest hit and supported her until the day she died (even though they were divorced, and he was married to Julie London and their kids were grown).

I always tell my students that when in doubt, be generous with their co-writers. If you two write well together, percentages shouldn't get in the way.

Winkler digresses yet again . . .
Burt Bacharach and Hal David had a big falling out when Burt, who arranged and produced all the music, asked for a bigger share of the royalty from their monumental musical flop, Lost Horizon. *Hal said no and the pair didn't write together for many years after their split and never really had the success they had prior to when they reunited.*

Making a formal contract with the percentages spelled out is critical. It may cost you a couple of hundred dollars in lawyer's fees, but it could save you a lot of aggravation down the line. Note: I've spent a lot of money on lawyers in my career and I've never regretted it once.

HOW ABOUT GIVING AWAY YOUR PUBLISHING OR A PERCENTAGE OF IT?

I'm not against giving away a percentage of your publishing. However, you need to have the publisher spell out clearly what they can be expected to do to earn that percentage. I find most songwriters aren't excellent songpluggers (promoters of their songs)—artists and savvy businesspeople are two separate entities (usually). However, try to get a term limit for your song to be tied up with the publisher. Because no matter how excited the publisher is about the song, the hottest period to get it covered by an artist or placed in a media situation is in the first couple of months the publisher has it. I prefer contracts that spell out that the publisher has it for just one or two years at the max. To give a publisher publishing, they must give you something in return, or the credible promise with a timeline of such.

This is a good discussion to have with your cowriter. A very important point: each cowriter controls whether they can assign their percentage of the song to a publisher. There's a certain ilk of writer who never wants to do that, and they can be very frustrating. However, in my humble opinion, an agreed upon percent of something is worth far more than 100 percent of nothing.

In the ever-changing world of songwriting, songs are being written in different configurations. One of the most popular is "toplining," which is essentially writing a vocal part over a premade music bed. If someone hires you to do toplining, they've already created the music or the beat and you will be expected to write the rest (see page 69).

The producer/arranger then shares in the writer's credit of the tune. Since there is recording software that can be accessed in a home studio or even your phone, the sophisticated arrangements needed for a pop song to be a hit can be done quickly. The producer/writer can give you a track, beats, or a whole arrangement that sounds great, often before the lyrics and melody of the song have been written. This has many positives, if the track is good, it immediately puts you in the genre and the groove you need to be in, which is no small thing.

COPYRIGHTING YOUR SONG

Here's how to copyright your song. Make an MP3 of the song and upload it to the U.S. government copyright website: https://www.copyright.gov/. Or you can upload an individual "lead sheet" (melody line, lyrics, and chords) of the song. You can copyright a single song on a "standard application" or, to save some money, you can register up to ten unpublished works on a single application (but you must select a "group of unpublished works"). (For current fees check the U.S. Copyright Office website: https://www.copyright.gov/forms/formpa.pdf.

Here are the forms:

Copyright Office fees are subject to change. For current fees, check the Copyright Office website at www.copyright.gov, write the Copyright Office, or call (202) 707-3000 or 1-877-476-0778 (toll free).

Clear Form

Form PA
For a Work of Performing Arts
UNITED STATES COPYRIGHT OFFICE
REGISTRATION NUMBER

_____
PA   PAU
EFFECTIVE DATE OF REGISTRATION

_____ _____ _____
Month   Day   Year

Privacy Act Notice: Sections 408-410 of title 17 of the *United States Code* authorize the Copyright Office to collect the personally identifying information requested on this form in order to process the application for copyright registration. By providing this information you are agreeing to routine uses of the information that include publication to give legal notice of your copyright claim as required by 17 U.S.C. §705. It will appear in the Office's online catalog. If you do not provide the information requested, registration may be refused or delayed, and you may not be entitled to certain relief, remedies, and benefits under the copyright law.

DO NOT WRITE ABOVE THIS LINE. IF YOU NEED MORE SPACE, USE A SEPARATE CONTINUATION SHEET.

---

1 TITLE OF THIS WORK ▼

PREVIOUS OR ALTERNATIVE TITLES ▼

NATURE OF THIS WORK ▼ See instructions

---

2 a NAME OF AUTHOR ▼

DATES OF BIRTH AND DEATH
Year Born ▼   Year Died ▼

Was this contribution to the work a "work made for hire"?
☐ Yes
☐ No

AUTHOR'S NATIONALITY OR DOMICILE
Name of Country
OR { Citizen of _____
     Domiciled in _____

WAS THIS AUTHOR'S CONTRIBUTION TO THE WORK
Anonymous?   ☐ Yes ☐ No
Pseudonymous? ☐ Yes ☐ No
If the answer to either of these questions is "Yes," see detailed instructions.

NATURE OF AUTHORSHIP Briefly describe nature of material created by this author in which copyright is claimed. ▼

NOTE
Under the law, the "author" of a "work made for hire" is generally the employer, not the employee (see instructions). For any part of this work that was "made for hire" check "Yes" in the space provided, give the employer (or other person for whom the work was prepared) as "Author" of that part, and leave the space for dates of birth and death blank.

b NAME OF AUTHOR ▼

DATES OF BIRTH AND DEATH
Year Born ▼   Year Died ▼

Was this contribution to the work a "work made for hire"?
☐ Yes
☐ No

AUTHOR'S NATIONALITY OR DOMICILE
Name of Country
OR { Citizen of _____
     Domiciled in _____

WAS THIS AUTHOR'S CONTRIBUTION TO THE WORK
Anonymous?   ☐ Yes ☐ No
Pseudonymous? ☐ Yes ☐ No
If the answer to either of these questions is "Yes," see detailed instructions.

NATURE OF AUTHORSHIP Briefly describe nature of material created by this author in which copyright is claimed. ▼

c NAME OF AUTHOR ▼

DATES OF BIRTH AND DEATH
Year Born ▼   Year Died ▼

Was this contribution to the work a "work made for hire"?
☐ Yes
☐ No

AUTHOR'S NATIONALITY OR DOMICILE
Name of Country
OR { Citizen of _____
     Domiciled in _____

WAS THIS AUTHOR'S CONTRIBUTION TO THE WORK
Anonymous?   ☐ Yes ☐ No
Pseudonymous? ☐ Yes ☐ No
If the answer to either of these questions is "Yes," see detailed instructions.

NATURE OF AUTHORSHIP Briefly describe nature of material created by this author in which copyright is claimed. ▼

---

3 a YEAR IN WHICH CREATION OF THIS WORK WAS COMPLETED This information must be given ONLY if this work Year in all cases.

b DATE AND NATION OF FIRST PUBLICATION OF THIS PARTICULAR WORK
Complete this information Month _____ Day _____ Year _____
has been published.   Nation

---

4 COPYRIGHT CLAIMANT(S) Name and address must be given even if the claimant is the same as the author given in space 2. ▼

See instructions before completing this space

TRANSFER If the claimant(s) named here in space 4 is (are) different from the author(s) named in space 2, give a brief statement of how the claimant(s) obtained ownership of the copyright. ▼

APPLICATION RECEIVED

ONE DEPOSIT RECEIVED

TWO DEPOSITS RECEIVED

FUNDS RECEIVED

DO NOT WRITE HERE
OFFICE USE ONLY

MORE ON BACK ▶   • Complete all applicable spaces (numbers 5-9) on the reverse side of this page.
• See detailed instructions.   • Sign the form at line 8.

DO NOT WRITE HERE
Page 1 of _____ pages

EXAMINED BY	FORM PA
CHECKED BY	
☐ CORRESPONDENCE Yes	FOR COPYRIGHT OFFICE USE ONLY

DO NOT WRITE ABOVE THIS LINE. IF YOU NEED MORE SPACE, USE A SEPARATE CONTINUATION SHEET.

PREVIOUS REGISTRATION Has registration for this work, or for an earlier version of this work, already been made in the Copyright Office?
☐ Yes ☐ No If your answer is "Yes," why is another registration being sought? (Check appropriate box.) ▼ If your answer is No, do not check box A, B, or C.
a. ☐ This is the first published edition of a work previously registered in unpublished form.
b. ☐ This is the first application submitted by this author as copyright claimant.
c. ☐ This is a changed version of the work, as shown by space 6 on this application.
If your answer is "Yes," give Previous Registration Number ▼ Year of Registration ▼

5

DERIVATIVE WORK OR COMPILATION Complete both space 6a and 6b for a derivative work; complete only 6b for a compilation.
Preexisting Material Identify any preexisting work or works that this work is based on or incorporates. ▼

a

6

See instructions before completing this space.

Material Added to This Work Give a brief, general statement of the material that has been added to this work and in which copyright is claimed. ▼

b

DEPOSIT ACCOUNT If the registration fee is to be charged to a Deposit Account established in the Copyright Office, give name and number of Account.
Name ▼   Account Number ▼

a

7

CORRESPONDENCE Give name and address to which correspondence about this application should be sent. Name/Address/Apt/City/State/Zip ▼

b

Area code and daytime telephone number (   )   Fax number (   )
Email

CERTIFICATION* I, the undersigned, hereby certify that I am the
Check only one ▶
☐ author
☐ other copyright claimant
☐ owner of exclusive right(s)
☐ authorized agent of _____
Name of author or other copyright claimant, or owner of exclusive right(s) ▲

8

of the work identified in this application and that the statements made by me in this application are correct to the best of my knowledge.

Typed or printed name and date ▼ If this application gives a date of publication in space 3, do not sign and submit it before that date.
_____ Date _____

Signature (X) ▼
X _____

Certificate will be mailed in window envelope to this address:	Name ▼ Number/Street/Apt ▼ City/State/Zip ▼	**YOU MUST:** • Complete all necessary spaces • Sign your application in space 8 **SEND ALL 3 ELEMENTS** **IN THE SAME PACKAGE:** 1. Application form 2. Nonrefundable filing fee in check or money order payable to *U.S. Copyright Office* 3. Deposit material **MAIL TO:** Library of Congress Copyright Office-PA 101 Independence Avenue SE Washington, DC 20559-6000

9

*17 U.S.C. §506(e): Any person who knowingly makes a false representation of a material fact in the application for copyright registration provided for by section 409, or in any written statement filed in connection with the application, shall be fined not more than $2,500.

Form PA—Full Printed: 05/2019 Printed on recycled paper

Copyright Office fees are subject to change. For current fees, check the Copyright Office website at www.copyright.gov, write the Copyright Office, or call (202) 707-3000 or 1-877-476-0778 (toll free).

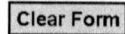

Form SR
For a Sound Recording
UNITED STATES COPYRIGHT OFFICE

REGISTRATION NUMBER

SR   SRU

EFFECTIVE DATE OF REGISTRATION

Month   Day   Year

Privacy Act Notice: Sections 408-410 of title 17 of the *United States Code* authorize the Copyright Office to collect the personally identifying information requested on this form in order to process the application for copyright registration. By providing this information you are agreeing to routine uses of the information that include publication to give legal notice of your copyright claim as required by 17 U.S.C. §705. It will appear in the Office's online catalog. If you do not provide the information requested, registration may be refused or delayed, and you may not be entitled to certain relief, remedies, and benefits under the copyright law.

DO NOT WRITE ABOVE THIS LINE. IF YOU NEED MORE SPACE, USE A SEPARATE CONTINUATION SHEET.

1 TITLE OF THIS WORK ▼

PREVIOUS, ALTERNATIVE, OR CONTENTS TITLES (CIRCLE ONE) ▼

2 a NAME OF AUTHOR ▼

DATES OF BIRTH AND DEATH
Year Born ▼   Year Died ▼

Was this contribution to the work a "work made for hire"?
☐ Yes
☐ No

AUTHOR'S NATIONALITY OR DOMICILE
Name of Country
OR { Citizen of ▶
     Domiciled in ▶

WAS THIS AUTHOR'S CONTRIBUTION TO THE WORK
Anonymous? ☐ Yes ☐ No
Pseudonymous? ☐ Yes ☐ No

If the answer to either of these questions is "Yes," see detailed instructions.

NATURE OF AUTHORSHIP Briefly describe nature of material created by this author in which copyright is claimed. ▼

NOTE
Under the law, the "author" of a "work made for hire" is generally the employer, not the employee (see instructions). For any part of this work that was "made for hire," check "Yes" in the space provided, give the employer (or other person for whom the work was prepared) as "Author" of that part, and leave the space for dates of birth and death blank.

b NAME OF AUTHOR ▼

DATES OF BIRTH AND DEATH
Year Born ▼   Year Died ▼

Was this contribution to the work a "work made for hire"?
☐ Yes
☐ No

AUTHOR'S NATIONALITY OR DOMICILE
Name of Country
OR { Citizen of ▶
     Domiciled in ▶

WAS THIS AUTHOR'S CONTRIBUTION TO THE WORK
Anonymous? ☐ Yes ☐ No
Pseudonymous? ☐ Yes ☐ No

If the answer to either of these questions is "Yes," see detailed instructions.

NATURE OF AUTHORSHIP Briefly describe nature of material created by this author in which copyright is claimed. ▼

c NAME OF AUTHOR ▼

DATES OF BIRTH AND DEATH
Year Born ▼   Year Died ▼

Was this contribution to the work a "work made for hire"?
☐ Yes
☐ No

AUTHOR'S NATIONALITY OR DOMICILE
Name of Country
OR { Citizen of ▶
     Domiciled in ▶

WAS THIS AUTHOR'S CONTRIBUTION TO THE WORK
Anonymous? ☐ Yes ☐ No
Pseudonymous? ☐ Yes ☐ No

If the answer to either of these questions is "Yes," see detailed instructions.

NATURE OF AUTHORSHIP Briefly describe nature of material created by this author in which copyright is claimed. ▼

3 a YEAR IN WHICH CREATION OF THIS WORK WAS COMPLETED
Year ▶   This information must be given in all cases.

b DATE AND NATION OF FIRST PUBLICATION OF THIS PARTICULAR WORK
Complete this information ONLY if this work has been published.
Month ▶   Day ▶   Year ▶
Nation ▶

4 a COPYRIGHT CLAIMANT(S) Name and address must be given even if the claimant is the same as the author given in space 2. ▼

APPLICATION RECEIVED

ONE DEPOSIT RECEIVED

TWO DEPOSITS RECEIVED

FUNDS RECEIVED

See instructions before completing this space.

b TRANSFER If the claimant(s) named here in space 4 is (are) different from the author(s) named in space 2, give a brief statement of how the claimant(s) obtained ownership of the copyright. ▼

MORE ON BACK ▶
• Complete all applicable spaces (numbers 5-9) on the reverse side of this page.
• See detailed instructions.
• Sign the form at line 8.

DO NOT WRITE HERE
Page 1 of _____ pages

EXAMINED BY	FORM SR
CHECKED BY	
CORRESPONDENCE ☐ Yes	FOR COPYRIGHT OFFICE USE ONLY

DO NOT WRITE ABOVE THIS LINE. IF YOU NEED MORE SPACE, USE A SEPARATE CONTINUATION SHEET.

PREVIOUS REGISTRATION Has registration for this work, or for an earlier version of this work, already been made in the Copyright Office?
☐ Yes ☐ No If your answer is "Yes," why is another registration being sought? (Check appropriate box) ▼
a. ☐ This work was previously registered in unpublished form and now has been published for the first time.
b. ☐ This is the first application submitted by this author as copyright claimant.
c. ☐ This is a changed version of the work, as shown by space 6 on this application.
If your answer is "Yes," give: Previous Registration Number ▼   Year of Registration ▼

5

DERIVATIVE WORK OR COMPILATION
Preexisting Material Identify any preexisting work or works that this work is based on or incorporates. ▼

a

Material Added to This Work Give a brief, general statement of the material that has been added to this work and in which copyright is claimed. ▼

b

6

See instructions before completing this space.

DEPOSIT ACCOUNT If the registration fee is to be charged to a deposit account established in the Copyright Office, give name and number of account.
Name ▼   Account Number ▼

a

CORRESPONDENCE Give name and address to which correspondence about this application should be sent. Name/Address/Apt/City/State/Zip ▼

b
Area code and daytime telephone number (   )   Fax number (   )
Email

7

CERTIFICATION* I, the undersigned, hereby certify that I am the
Check only one ▼
☐ author   ☐ owner of exclusive right(s)
☐ other copyright claimant   ☐ authorized agent of _____
                                Name of author or other copyright claimant, or owner of exclusive right(s) ▲

of the work identified in this application and that the statements made by me in this application are correct to the best of my knowledge.

Typed or printed name and date ▼ If this application gives a date of publication in space 3, do not sign and submit it before that date.

_____ Date _____

Signature ▼

8

Certificate will be mailed in window envelope to this address:	Name ▼ Number/Street/Apt ▼ City/State/Zip ▼	**YOU MUST:** · Complete all necessary spaces · Sign your application in space 8 **SEND ALL 3 ELEMENTS IN THE SAME PACKAGE:** 1. Application form 2. Nonrefundable filing fee in check or money order payable to *U.S. Copyright Office* 3. Deposit material **MAIL TO:** Library of Congress U.S. Copyright Office-SR 101 Independence Avenue SE Washington, DC 20559-6000

9

*17 U.S.C. §506(e): Any person who knowingly makes a false representation of a material fact in the application for copyright registration provided for by section 409, or in any written statement filed in connection with the application, shall be fined not more than $2,500.

Form SR-Full   Rev: 05/2019   Printed on recycled paper

27
FINAL REVIEW

You're almost at the end of the book. You've done the Songwriting Actions and hopefully rewritten The Beatles' "Penny Lane," written a lyric based on the elements in a painting, and built a house (*I mean a song*) with the techniques, tips, and craft contained in this book. This final review will let you know how much of the information you have retained and, perhaps, which chapters you need to review. Learning to write a song is a lifelong process—one that only gets better and more rewarding the more you write—so have a little patience, definitely have a little fun, and say what only you can say.

FINAL REVIEW QUESTIONS
1. Name two ways to maintain the structure and scansion of the tune when you start with the lyric first.
2. What are the two major forms of songwriting today?
3. What are two different types of rhymes: one from the Great American Songbook era and one primarily being used in today's popular music?
4. What are at least three things you must do in a verse?
5. Should you create and maintain a title folder on your phone or computer?
6. True or false: When writing a musical, the songs should always further the story?
7. Explain the concept of "show, don't tell."

8. When you're writing a lyric for a high note, do you end it with an open vowel or a consonant?
9. Should a lyric be conversational? And what does that mean?
10. What are at least three things you need to do in a chorus?
11. Name a popular AABA song other than "Don't Know Why."
12. Is "time" and "mine" a perfect rhyme?
13. What is a gatekeeper and why do you need them?
14. What does "write to title" mean?
15. Are "parrot and carrot" an imperfect rhyme?
16. What are at least three things you must do in a bridge?
17. What's anaphora?
18. What's a picture title?
19. What are three things happening in music today? (Subject to change as music evolves.)
20. What are three things not happening in music today? (Subject to change as music evolves.)
21. When writing to an existing melody, what is the first thing you need to do as a lyricist?
22. What are several ways to come up with a great title?
23. Does a bridge ever follow a second verse?
24. When you're performing, what should you always do to capture your performance?

ANSWERS TO FINAL REVIEW

1. You can come up with a "dummy melody," which is a melody you create after you've written a few lines or the whole verse. It does not have to be good. It is there just to give you the scansion of the line and the form of the song, or you can write a lyric to an existing melody. All you have to know is what the form of the song is so you know where to put (insert *or* place) your title. See chapter 11.
2. Verse/chorus and AABA. See chapter 5.
3. Perfect (Great American Songbook) and imperfect rhymes (popular songs)—also known as false, or bastard rhyming. Perfect is where the vowel and the consonant match, for example, "blue" and "shoe," and imperfect rhyming is where either the vowel or the consonants don't match, for example, "blue" and "shoes." See chapter 9.

4. So many to choose from! Set up the story. Who's singing, who are they singing to? What are they trying to accomplish in the song? Setting up the rhyme scheme and scansion of the song. Also, indicating time of day and location can be helpful. See chapter 5.
5. Yes, you should always have a title folder. See chapter 4.
6. True. Since the musicals *Showboat* and *Oklahoma!*, musical theater songs have served to further the story. See chapter 17.
7. It's a wonderful songwriting device that lets the listener discover the emotion and action the song is conveying. When you *tell* your listener, "she just broke my heart" or "my heart is filled with happiness," they already know the answer. However, if you use three elements—*action*, *imagery*, and *detail*—you can tell your audience a story. So, instead of writing "you left me, and my heart is broken," write, "I saw you sneaking out the door with your suitcase and a plane ticket, and when the door shut, I tried to sleep but couldn't stop crying." (The latter sentence is "showing" us rather than "telling" us.) See chapters 19 and 23.
8. When writing a lyric for a high note, always make sure that the syllable on which the high note falls is on an open vowel. Just listen to any Celine Dion or Ariana Grande tune. "Let It Go" from *Frozen* is a good example. See chapter 7.
9. A lyric should be conversational, because basically your job as a lyricist is to tell the listener a story and conversation is the natural mode of doing that. Fancy multisyllabic words and obscure similes are awkward and only hinder perceiving the story. See chapters 7 and 23.
10. The chorus is where you put the title of the song. It's usually in the first or last line of the chorus. It can be in every line, and it should appear in the chorus at least twice. It should vary both in rhyme scheme and scansion from the verse. It should be higher melodically than the verse. It should sum up what the song is about—and not continue or develop the story. It should be so memorable that your audience should be able to sing it back. See chapter 5.
11. So many! "Unforgettable," "Every Breath You Take," "The Way We Were," and "Over the Rainbow," "Hey, Delilah," and "Popular" from the hit musical *Wicked* are more current examples. But definitely in pop, hip-hop, and country it is not used much, if at all. See chapter 5.

12. No. The "m" in "time" and the "n" in "mine" don't match. However, this type of imperfect rhyme is used frequently in today's music and is found in one of my favorite lyrics of all time. In "Wichita Lineman" by Jimmy Webb—"And I need you more than want you, and I want you for all *time*, but the Wichita lineman is still on the *line*." See chapter 9.
13. A gatekeeper is someone who is further along than you in the business or in a position to be able to judge and guide you as a songwriter. If you are in a songwriter community you can go to the most accomplished writer in the group, or if you take lessons it could be your teacher or a respected critic, publisher, manager, or lawyer who works with songwriters and singers. It is not your significant other or parent. It's someone who doesn't have something to lose by being honest with you. You need three gatekeepers. Play them one or two songs and take them out to lunch or pay for their time. It is well worth it. See chapter 16.
14. That means that your story/plot should reflect your title. If you're writing a song called "Born to Lose," you shouldn't write a second verse about how you've just met the greatest girl in the world. Everything in the song should reinforce and amplify the title. See chapter 9.
15. No, the vowels and consonants in "parrot" and "carrot" match perfectly, therefore, it's not an imperfect rhyme. See hapter 9.
16. A bridge is the changeup. You can change the person or the timeframe. In the bridge, you definitely want the scansion and the rhyme scheme to be different than all the other sections of the tune. Generally, the last half of the bridge builds to the chorus, both melodically and phrase-wise. It helps further the story, look at the story from a different angle, or give the philosophy of the song. See chapter 5.
17. Anaphora is a repetitive device where you repeat the first couple of words in each successive line. It's a little hook and a way of organizing the lyric, that is, "I wish you bluebirds in the spring," "I wish you health, but more than wealth, I wish you love." See chapters 11 and 23.
18. A picture title is a title that when you say it, you see it. For example, "Flowers" by Miley Cyrus, "Vampire" by Olivia Rodrigo, and "Castle on the Hill" by Ed Sheeran. See chapter 4.
19. Rap/vocal collaborations, post-choruses, imperfect rhyming, sparse production, rap-influenced phrasing in the verses, eighties techno tracks. (Subject to change as music evolves.)

20. Rock bands, sax solos, whistling, trumpet solos, acoustic instruments, folk songs. (Subject to change as music evolves.)
21. The first thing you need to figure out is what's the form of the melody. It will tell you where you need to place your title. See chapter 14.
22. Old movie titles, book titles, listening to people talk in coffee shops, lines from movies or TV shows, that is, "You had me at hello." See chapter 4.
23. No. See chapter 5.
24. Video or voice memo your performance to see which songs get the most applause and what you are doing right and wrong as a singer/performer. See chapter 15.

28
WHAT DO I DO NOW?

So, you've reached the end of the various chapters' Songwriter Actions and completed the final review. Congratulations! You're feeling really good about the songs you've been writing, and you've done these three things:

1. Played your songs for your three "gatekeepers" and been told they're wonderful.
2. You've played them at some open mic nights and the crowd reaction has been good/great, and you have the videos to prove it.
3. You've received some good feedback on the songs in classes or songwriting groups.

Good news, bad news . . .
First, the bad news.
　　The days when you could take your songs to a publisher on L.A.'s Sunset Boulevard or on Tin Pan Alley in New York are essentially gone. Except for Nashville, which is still a songwriter's town, this is not necessarily the best way to get your songs covered. Publishers, managers, lawyers, and labels are looking for the whole package. They want everything: great song, great singer, great producers, and great production all neatly wrapped and presented to them with one hundred thousand X and Instagram followers and a heavy presence on Spotify.

Here's the good news.

The best way for you to get your songs covered is to become a producer too.

At this time, I wouldn't blame you for thinking, "Shoot. Being a songwriter is hard enough and now I've got one more job to deal with." I understand, but the producer's job is very closely aligned with writing the song. That's just a fact.

Producers control all aspects of the recording process. They pick the material with the artist (which in this case will be your material). Then, they make sure they get the best arrangements and players to support the singer. They literally direct the singer's vocals and when that's done, they work with the engineer on the mix of the song (or, if they're also an engineer, they mix the song). As the producer, you are guarding your baby—the song—at every step and maximizing its chance of success.

Now, if you're not a "techie" (and believe me, I'm not), you already know it. What you've got to do is align yourself with someone who is, and who owns or has access to a home studio. A lot of technical talents are great with sounds, but perhaps not so good with words, song forms, and hooks. They need you! With the right partners, you can form a production team, like Bruno Mars. His team called themselves the Smeezingtons and it consisted of Mars, Philip Lawrence, and Ari Levine. Their production and writing services were in demand from 2009 until their breakup in 2015. Casey Musgrave produced her 2019 GRAMMY Album of the Year *Golden Hour* with fellow songwriters Daniel Tashian and Ian Fitchuk. The big daddy of the last thirty-plus years is Sweden's Max Martin, who has written or cowritten twenty-five-plus *Billboard* Hot 100 number one songs, most of which he has also produced or coproduced for artists ranging from Britney Spears to The Weeknd. Every Beyoncé, Justin Bieber, and Ariana Grande album has most, if not all, the tracks produced by producer/writing teams.

You're not going to get to these megastars out of the box. Everyone is trying to get to them and they are all fairly inaccessible behind a wall of agents, managers, and lawyers. So, what do you do? You find an artist who can really do justice to your material. Sometimes that artist can be yourself, but be honest and ask yourself if you're the best vehicle to sell your songs.

Superstar producers such as Shane McAnally, Benny Blanco, the aforementioned Max Martin, and Pharrell Williams all started as artists. Practically everybody in the music business started out wanting to be an artist but discovered that they weren't good enough or cute enough or hungry enough or maybe they just aged out of contention. As it stands now in pop, hip-hop, and urban music, you've got to be in your early twenties to be viable.

So, how do you find an artist?

Miranda Lambert or Ed Sheeran may be unattainable, so set your sights a little more realistically. Get some notches on your belt with indie cuts by talented and lesser-known singers. Look for artists in your genre with a good local or regional following. They may not be packing arenas (yet!), but they might be getting people into the smaller clubs and bars. I remember when Katy Perry was playing the smallish Hotel Café in Hollywood, and everybody knew it was only a matter of time until she was going to make it. You want to be there when they're still lesser known.

GO TO LIVE SHOWS IN YOUR AREA

In your towns or adjacent cities, you'll find nightclubs and coffeehouses. These serve a couple of purposes: First, becoming a regular helps you get to know the artists you're pitching. Maybe you thought you had the perfect song for them, but after seeing their act, you realize you have another song that would be better. The songs they sing and their patter between songs are all clues as to the best material to offer them.

Second, it always helps to make things "personal." The music business is a "people's" business. If you can actually stare into someone's eyes, shake their hand, tell them how great they are, they probably won't forget you. It's great to put a face to a message. And like most things, when you're "on the scene," over time, people and opportunities will present themselves.

I'm a big believer in going to open mics and showcases for hot, but lesser-known, talents and then making a point of introducing myself. However, meeting performers before a show is always dicey. I usually wait until after the show. I position myself close to the stage to be the first one they can talk to—and lay back and take in the scene. Pick up on the cues the artist gives you. If the show went great and the musicians are all high-fiving and the performer seems happy, go for it! But if after the show the performer is grimacing and in the middle of a heated discussion with their keyboard player, perhaps wait until another time.

Winkler digresses . . .

Quite a few years ago I was at Catalina's, one of the foremost jazz clubs in Los Angeles, taking in the great saxophonist Joshua Redman. I wanted to meet him because I had just written lyrics (with a lovely cowriter named Lori Barth) for two of his instrumentals and he and his management had approved them. I was over the moon, and I wanted to thank him. Well, Joshua is a young, handsome guy, and when his dynamite set ended, his mind was definitely on connecting with a beautiful girl in the front row who was obviously quite smitten with him. After the set, I ignored all signals (and there were plenty) and thrust myself between them. And friends, it wasn't pretty. I can't blame Joshua; she was hot, and he was young and fancy-free. Just keep your eyes open.

The overall modus operandi when meeting a performer is to be polite, respectful, enthusiastic, and don't be pushy!

KNOW YOUR BUSINESS

If you are not in a major music metropolis like L.A., New York, Chicago, Atlanta, San Francisco, or Nashville, or can't easily travel to one, you might have to resort to emails and messaging. But be smart about it. Always do your homework on the artist. Spend time studying their websites and social media and become familiar with their music on streaming services. Listen to their most-played songs, read their bios, and really get a sense of what they're about. SoundCloud and similar formats let you search artists by genre and city, so you can find those with whom you feel you can really connect. Then send them a polite message, keeping the self-hype and amazing adjectives to a minimum, but including any achievements that would give you credibility. Then ask them if you can send them one or two songs. Promptly send them using Reelcrafter, DISCO.ac, or SoundCloud (I'll talk more about these later in this chapter).

Winkler digresses . . .

When sending your songs, I'm a stickler about lyric sheets. They should have the title of the song at the top, then the music and lyric writers and copyright symbol and publishing information. Also, label the sections of the song with verse, chorus, bridge, etc. Keep them looking professional and legible; don't go overboard with graphics or distracting fonts.

After an artist agrees to consider your material, just send one or two songs. (If they get more than three, the odds are they won't listen to them.) If the artist turns you down, or more than likely doesn't respond, don't pester them. You want to build a relationship for the future. Wait about ten days and send a nice follow-up, thanking them for listening to the tune or asking them if they've listened to the tune. And then leave it at that.

MOVE TO A MAJOR MUSIC METROPOLIS
If you're really serious about this songwriter thing, you need to be where the action and the people are. Make it happen.

NETWORK, NETWORK, NETWORK
When you're in the music capitals, there are plenty of showcases, open mics, and industry events sponsored by the performing rights and other professional organizations. Take advantage of them all. It's a process that may not get results immediately, but the more you attend, the more you'll see the landscape of the arena you're in and the people who populate it. Then, little by little, you'll form connections and relationships. The music world isn't that big!!!

Dan Kimpel, who's a great guy, author, interviewer, and columnist for *Music Connection* magazine is a songwriter's best friend (he's always been so helpful to me). He has even written a book about it called *Networking in the Music Business*. I remember a lecture he gave a few years back where he said that when you first walk into a music event, there are two things you should *not* do: look for friends or people you know, or head for the nearest bar. Instead, slow down, lay back, go to the edge of the room, and quietly observe what's going on. That way you can scope out what's really happening in the room, which is great advice that I will use forever. You're a writer, you're observant, so take the time to observe!

You'll see a lot of insightful things: music event staffers trailing the big shots, songwriters that look lost and may be drinking too much, songwriters high-fiving buddies they know and, of course, the lost souls toying with their phones, totally missing what's in front of them. You'll also soon see where the important people are holding court—animated, laughing with a mob of people hanging onto their every utterance. Listen for a minute to see if they're just blowhards or actually in an interactive conversation. Perhaps, while you're observing the room, you suddenly see the president of a major music publishing company and he's alone. What a break; get yourself over there. Once again, be enthusiastic, professional, and scope out his mood. Don't be pushy. And if you know a little something about him and his roster of writers, compliment him on a song that he publishes that you just love, but don't pick the obvious one. He'll love it. We all love being recognized for our good work and smarts. Be collegial and respectful, not obsequious and above all, not pushy. If you don't feel confident doing this, role-play this kind of interaction with a willing colleague or friend.

MY TOP TEN WAYS TO GET YOUR SONGS IN FRONT OF THE INDUSTRY

1. Durango Music Festival. This three-day conference, held twice a year, is a great way for songwriters to meet and interact with industry professionals. It focuses on pop and country songs for sync licensing. It includes panels, industry listening sessions by pros, and showcases where singer/songwriters who are preselected can sing on Thursday and Friday nights. The ratio of attendees to industry professionals is three to one attendees, so it's a fairly intimate experience.
2. ASCAP Experience. Held once a year in Los Angeles, this event, which is only for ASCAP members, is a wonderful way for songwriters to get their music heard and to interact with publishers, songwriters, and other industry professionals. It includes in-depth conversations with major industry players, live song feedback from top publishers, and panels on different industry topics.
3. Nashville Songwriters Association International (NSAI). An organization that includes all genres of music and has branches in many cities in the United States. It services both pro and amateur songwriters. NSAI also lobbies Washington for songwriters' rights. Its members have monthly meetings where guest publishers, educators, lawyers, and pro songwriters speak and listen to the songwriters' new material and give feedback.
4. Tin Pan South Songwriters Festival. This huge festival in Nashville occurs once a year, taking place over five days and is sponsored by NSAI. It has panels of industry professionals and noted songwriters and a panel giving live song feedback. Tin Pan South holds concerts all over Nashville, with professional songwriters and new writers showcasing their material during the festival. It is an excellent place to network.

5. TAXI Music. An independent A+R service that submits material songwriters, artists, and composers have created for consideration by publishers, music supervisors, and music libraries. To be submitted, the writers must be members of TAXI, and their material must be first vetted and chosen by TAXI's staff of professional songwriters. There is a yearly fee for belonging to the organization and a small fee for each submission, but TAXI does not take royalties for the songs submitted and chosen.
6. TAXI Road Rally. An annual weekend gathering gratis for TAXI members and open to paying guests. It connects its members with industry professionals, supervisors, other songwriters, and music libraries. It features panels, individual mentoring sessions, and members are eligible to be preselected to perform their songs on songwriter performance nights.
7. SoundCloud. An online audio streaming and distribution platform that allows users to upload, promote, and share their music. It's easy to use and you can send your music to industry professionals by sending them a link to your particular track or playlist.
8. Reelcrafter. A platform to present your songs for film and TV sync opportunities. It is easy to use, you can organize the look of your page, and use playlists or "reels" and descriptions to make your music searchable by industry professionals. It is easily accessed; all you need to do is send a link. There is a monthly fee to be on the site and to use its services.
9. DISCO.ac. Another platform to present your songs for film and TV sync opportunities. You can store and organize your music in one clear storage space, which means no hassling with files and folders. You can customize the look of your page to suit the style of music that you are showcasing. You can also track and monitor your analytics. And best of all, people to whom you are sending material can access it from any device by using a link that you've sent. There is a monthly fee to be on the site and to use its services.
10. Hotel Café. This is the premiere club in Los Angeles for new singer/songwriters specializing in acoustic-based music to perform. Industry professionals and music enthusiasts use this club as a source for finding new artists. It's been open since 2004 and it has launched the careers of Katy Perry, Ingrid Michaelson, and Sara Bareilles.

In New York City, the New York Songwriters Circle that has been around since 1991, is a respected live showcase for young songwriters starting out in the music business. It meets once a month at the Bitter End in the West Village. Such writers as Lana Del Rey, Hugh Prestwood, and Gavin DeGraw have gotten their start there.

Here are some final thoughts and tips.

1. Always put your best song first.
2. Don't be too proud. If your mother knows a big producer, meet them. We all need a lucky break once in a while. Use any connections or advantages you may have.
3. Subscribe to musicconnection.com and billboard.com. You need to know what's happening in the industry and who the players are.
4. All you need is for one person to say yes. Show business is mostly a "no" business. Remember, even Capitol Records turned down The Beatles at first.
5. Write with other people who are better than you are, whenever possible.
6. Keep your day job; being poor takes creativity away faster than anything.
7. Know where you fit. Know your strengths, weaknesses, and your sweet spots. You can't be all things to all people, and we live in a world of specialists. All you need is for the right people to truly like the real you.
8. Don't be jealous of another's success. If people in your songwriting group are making it before you, view it as a sign that you're next and you'll probably be right. People of a certain quality stick together and it means you are doing something right.
9. Keep up on current music and technology; don't be left behind.
10. Be nice. Be somebody other people want to hang out with. Writing songs is a collaborative process, mostly done by two or three people in a small room in close proximity to each other.

Winkler digresses . . .

Martin Page, who's cowritten such songs as "We Built This City" and "These Dreams," once spoke to my songwriting class and mentioned that one of the chief reasons he's had success is that artists and songwriters generally liked

WHAT DO I DO NOW?

Mark with Allee Willis when she spoke to his lyric writing class (photo by Mark Winkler).

him. He was fun to work with, cooperative, didn't have a big ego, and was a hard worker. Be the person with whom you'd want to write.

The late, great Allee Willis spoke to my class a few years back and I asked her how she wrote with so many different people, like Earth Wind & Fire ("September"), Brenda Russell (the musical *The Color Purple*), and the

Rembrandts ("I'll Be There for You," the theme from the TV show *Friends*), and she said it was because people liked being with her. The day she spoke to my class was, unfortunately, the longest period of time I'd ever get to spend with her; she died much too early in 2019. She was so charismatic, smart, outrageous, and fun, I didn't want the party to stop! I know I was not alone—so here's to you Allee. Sometimes all you need is one day.

Allee Willis exemplified my definition of being a big success in show business. She, like everybody else, started out wanting to be a singer, with a Laura Nyro vibe (if you don't know who Laura Nyro is, look her up, you'll be glad you did) on her album *Childstar* for Epic Records in 1974. Then life happened, and she wound up being a singer, a hit songwriter with GRAMMY awards, a member of the Songwriters Hall of Fame, a Tony-nominated writer of a hit Broadway musical, a music video art director, a proud and out gay woman, an ardent supporter of the city of Detroit, a supporter of animal rights, and a great friend to many and an artist who painted and made motorized sculptures and ceramics. She was also a renowned hostess.

So, as I noted in chapter 2, I cannot promise you will have multiple hit records, a major performing career, or thunderous acclaim. However, I can promise you that if you know how to write a song, and can recognize a great song, there is a wonderful place in the industry for you.

Just think of Allee Willis. She didn't wind up being universally recognized or mobbed wherever she went, but her career took its own sky-high memorable path and she wound up being so much more! And to think she started out just wanting to be a superstar (how boring!).

Which brings me to a student of mine at the UCLA extension. Brandon Jordan had been in a quite successful punk band in the 2000s, *KillRadio* on Columbia Records. The band had broken up, he had subsequently battled and conquered his drug problems before he enrolled in my class. However, he still looked every inch the punk rocker and was very intense. To be honest, when I saw him sitting in the front row I thought to myself, "I don't know if he's going to go for all of my rules and regulations."

I couldn't have been more mistaken. At the end of the class, he brought me a present and we went out for coffee and have since become friends.

Brandon went on to release some fine solo records, and also works at a wonderful organization called Rock to Recovery that helps people heal and transform their lives through the powerful experience of writing, playing, and performing music.

A few years ago, I received this email from him:

Hey Mark, been a long time.

I just wanted to tell you thanks for all that you've taught me in the UCLA classes. The time has now come for me to teach people and a lot of what comes out of my mouth is the stuff you taught me.

I'm a music therapist now that goes to drug/alcohol treatment centers and facilitates fifteen groups a week. I come into a facility, talk to the clients about my story and how music plays such an important role in regulating our emotions in life, then, we get someone writing lyrics.

We've written over 220 songs so far . . . over 60 songs a week!

So, there are a ton of ex-junkies and tweakers out there using your "so I say" trick to write the chorus, and a lot of the time, we use your concept and "write to title." It's awesome to watch these people blossom in the groups, and 90% of them have no musical background.

Thanks for all you taught me man, it really helped me in my early sobriety and now I'm able to give back to others and share the love of songwriting for therapeutic values.

Brandon Jordan

The act of writing a song can change a life. It can alter a mind or touch a heart. I know, it's happened to me . . . and it may just happen to you. Now keep writing.

GLOSSARY

AABA form: The most popular form of songwriting during the Great American Songbook era (the twenties through the fifties). The first two "As" tell the story of the song and contain the title in either the first or last line of the "A." The bridge is a "change-up" with a different rhyme scheme and scansion (length of line and stresses).
Alliteration: Beginning each word in a line with the same letter. For example, "sweet summer sensation" or "big, blonde, and beautiful."
Americana: A musical genre that combines traditional musical styles including country, folk, and the blues. It is generally singer-songwriter oriented and played on acoustic instruments.
Anaphora: Starting the first part of each line in a verse or chorus with the same three or four words. It is a form of repetition, and makes the lines easier to remember.
Authentic: It means that your music, songs, and performance come from who you really are. Audiences can spot inauthenticity a mile away. For example, if you are a middle-class kid from the valley, don't create a persona where you're a gangsta from the hood.
Book, the: In the musical theater world, it is the script of the show. It contains the story of the show, all spoken dialogue, as well as the lyrics of the musical numbers.

Bridge: The change-up; the bridge builds to the last chorus—it's a change in pace and perspective. You can also put the philosophy of the tune in the bridge.

Cadence: The rhythm of the line.

Character song: A song that focuses on writing from the point of view of someone who isn't you. It means stepping into their shoes and even using their particular language to tell their story. You can also write it about a character from your point of view. Elton John became "Rocket Man" in his song, while Jason Isbell wrote about the damaged characters in his song "Elephant."

Chorus: The first part contains the title hook (generally the title) and summarization of the theme of the song. Often the second part (sometimes called "the post chorus") is a nonsense syllable (called a *vocable*). Choruses are generally higher melodically than the rest of the song.

Conversational: To write your song much like you are telling your story to a friend or lover. Making the lyrics flow in an easily understood and clear manner.

Crickets: What a performer hears in a club or concert hall when the audience isn't responding to his material. It's so quiet you can hear crickets.

Drishti: A Sanskrit word generally used in yoga to mean a specific point to lock your gaze upon while holding a pose.

Furniture: A term used by Nashville songwriters meaning specific nouns and verbs in a lyric that contains pictures.

Gatekeeper: Someone who has a little bit more knowledge than you at this point but has no hidden agendas. They are there to support you—but also to tell you if you're doing something wrong.

Genre: A style of music that songs fall into based on their similarities and adherence to certain musical rules. For example, a country song has different instrumentation, singing styles, vernacular, and story plot than someone doing a musical theater or rap song.

Good bones: A song that is written with a great foundation of melody and lyrics and song craft that gives the listener an emotional response. It is not necessarily dependent upon the production of the recording or the performance of the artist.

Great American Songbook: A group of songs generally written from the twenties to the mid-fifties. Such composers as George Gershwin, Cole Porter, and Irving Berlin were some of the most important composers at that time. These songs have lasted through the decades and are still being sung by such artists as Michael Bublé, John Pizzarelli, and a score of jazz and cabaret singers.

Home studio: A collection of equipment for recording music at home. With advanced computers and the price of recording equipment becoming more affordable, more artists and producers do a lot of their recording in their rebuilt garages or bedrooms, on their laptops, and even their smartphones.

Hook: Generally refers to the title of the song in the chorus, but it can be any part of the song that an audience remembers and likes. It can be the horns in Beyoncé's "Crazy in Love" or the descending bass line at the end of the chorus of "These Boots are Made for Walking" or the crazy string line in Britney Spears's "Toxic."

Karaoke tracks: Karaoke tracks refers to the tracks of the song minus the vocal, so you can sing over the instruments.

Laundry list song: This is a technique that can be used in any part of the song and in any genre. It is basically a list of things that tell the story of the song. It's a clever way to organize your song while lending it some repetition and "hookiness." For example, "Last Friday Night" by Katy Perry or "Royals" by Lorde.

Lead sheet: A musical notation of the essential elements of the song—the melody, lyrics, and chords.

Libretto: The script of an opera, but it can also mean the "book" of a musical.

Location songs: Songs that are set in one place. For example, "On Broadway" is set in New York City or "Havana" sung by Camila Cabello featuring Young Thug. You can use the details of the city to inform the lyric of the song.

Loops: A repeated musical section of sound material, usually drums or piano or guitar. Then, the player would trigger, then play along with the loop to fill out the arrangement.

Melody line: A series of notes forming a distinctive sequence. It's generally the most memorable part of the song—the part of the song that the singer sings.

Message song: A song that has a philosophy, lesson, or view to impart on the listener. For example: "Born This Way" by Lady Gaga or "Man in the Mirror" by Michael Jackson.

Metaphor: For example, raining cats and dogs; heart of gold.

Multisyllabic: Any word that has more than one syllable. As a lyricist, it is important to know if the word with many syllables is easy or difficult to sing.

You want everything to roll off the singer's tongue and sound pleasing to the ear.

Musician-proof charts: Charts that don't contain any sections or musical phrases that take an undue amount of time for the musicians to master. Especially important if you have limited rehearsal time or you are using new musicians on out of town gigs.

New Jack swing: Most popular in the eighties and popularized by producers Teddy Riley and Bernard Wright. It is a fusion genre of the rhythms and production techniques of hip-hop and dance pop. For example, "Don't Be Cruel" by Bobby Brown and "I Wanna Sex You Up" by Color Me Badd.

Onomatopoeia: The naming of a thing or an action by imitation of its natural sounds. For example, "buzz," "hiss, "zap," or "splat."

Open vowel: Often used on the end of the line of songs where the note is extended and goes high. For example, "A," "E," and "O." When you sing these vowels it's more natural and pleasing to the ear. The opposite is singing these notes on a closed consonant.

Out chorus: The final chorus returning after an instrumental section or bridge in a somewhat altered form. It could contain a call and response section, a contrapuntal section, or climax to the end in a dramatic fashion. For example, "Wind Beneath My Wings" by Bette Midler or "Man in the Mirror" by Michael Jackson.

Payoff line: The last line of the chorus that delivers a summation, a laugh, or a little emotional jolt. Almost like a punchline to a joke. For example, "These boots are made for walking and that's just what they'll do. [*Payoff line*] One of these days these boots are gonna walk all over you."

Philosophy song: Contains a lyric expressing a point of view about the world. For example, "As Time Goes By" or "What a Wonderful World."

Phrase throwing: It's a line that in and of itself is catchy, although it may not be so meaningful.

Picture words: Specific nouns and verbs that paint the scene in the song. In Nashville it's called "furniture."

Poppin': A style of bass playing in the eighties where the bassist wrenches the played string or strings away from the bass (or guitar) and let it twang hard against the fretboard upon release.

Post choruses: A relatively new development in songwriting. A second part of the chorus that contains a "vocable" or another hook.

Prosody: Where the lyric fits the melodic line in such a way that the lyrics catch the stresses and the shape of the melody for maximum ease in singing and comprehension of the audience.

Race music: Commercially recorded African American popular music from the early twentieth century including blues and jazz. Labels had their own sub-labels to sell this music.

Rap music: A genre of music that started in the Bronx in the early seventies by African American musicians. It involves rhythmic speech, rhyme, and street vernacular. While over fifty years old, it is still predominant and influential in pop music today.

Recitative: In opera and oratorio, the musicalized dialogue before the aria is sung. It is sung in the rhythm of ordinary speech with many words on the same note.

Refrain: In popular music it is the chorus or the lines that are repeated in a song.

Repetition: An important technique used in lyric writing. It can be the repetition of the title or a musical phrase, an instrumental figure or a few words in every line of the verse, for example, "I Hope You Dance" by Lee Ann Womack.

Rhyme:

    Perfect rhymes: A rhyme that has both the vowel and the consonant matching in the rhyming words. For example, "time" and "rhyme." It does not need to be spelled the same, but only sound the same.

    Imperfect rhymes: Almost rhymes, bastard rhyming, false rhymes, imperfect rhymes: A rhyme that has either the vowel or the consonant matching the rhyming word, but not both. For example, "blues" and "shoe" have the vowel sound matching, but the consonant sounds differing.

    One rhyme: Also known as a "masculine rhyme." It is a one-syllable word generally at the end of the line that rhymes with another one-syllable word. For example, "sky" and "fly."

    Double rhymes: Also known as "feminine rhymes." It is a two-syllable word (or two one-syllable words) generally at the end of the line that rhymes with another double or feminine rhyme. The rhyme is one syllable back. For example, "*trou*ble" and "*bub*ble."

Three-rhyme: Also known as a triple rhyme. It is a three-syllable word (or three words) generally at the end of the line that rhymes with another three-syllable word. For example, "*mys*tery" and "*his*tory."

Four rhyme: It is a four-syllable word (or four one-syllable words) generally at the end of the line. The rhyme is three syllables back. For example, "*care* where you are" and "*there* where you are."

Inner rhymes: It is a rhyme involving a word in the middle of a line and another at the end of the line.

Rhyme scheme: The ordered pattern of rhymes at the ends of the lines of a verse, chorus, or bridge.

Scansion: The rhythm and length of the line.

Show don't tell: A technique used in all forms of writing. You don't *tell* us what is happening in a song or what the character is feeling, you *show* it through pictures and action. For example: (*tell*) I'm happy and in love; (*show*) my heart is pumping and I'm walking nine feet off of the ground.

Simile: For example, stars like diamonds.

Singer-ese: A singer communicating with a musician by using the lyrics of the song instead of the musical terms that the musician is reading. For example, can we go back to the lyric "I love you baby" instead of the bar number, the repeat sign or any other part of the song that is notated on the music.

Song-plugger: Someone who looks for singers/groups to record your songs. Generally, they work for publishers.

Sound Files (MP3, MP4, WAV): The current standard for listening and sending songs is on sound files. It can be either sent as an email attachment or on WeTransfer or Dropbox or placed on SoundCloud.

SoundCloud: A music sharing website that allows its users to upload, promote, and share their songs.

Specificity: One of the most important techniques in song writing. Always using the most distinct way to describe a noun or verb. For example, instead of car use "Chevy" or "Escalade"; instead of walking, use "skipping" or "limping" or "racing."

Standard, A: A song with long staying power that has been recorded by a variety of artists over many years.

Sung-through: A musical, musical film, opera, or other work of performance art in which songs entirely, or almost entirely, stand in place of any spoken dialogue.

GLOSSARY

Syntax: The arrangement of words and phrases in a sentence.

Techno tracks: Generally found in EDM (Electronic Dance Music). They're played by synthesizers and the rhythm is typically in common time. They're very repetitive and hypnotic in nature.

Tentpole songs: Tunes that always get a great response when played live. Performers should weave them through their set to ensure they always have a song that will get a great audience response. If you do a new song and it doesn't go over, you'll always know that the tentpole song will win them over.

Title folder: A place where you keep titles, story/plots, and good lines for future songs. It can be on your laptop as a document, or on your phone in "Notes," or "old school" in a small notebook.

Toplining: Crafting a melody and lyric to a finished track given to you by the producer of the song.

Track(s): A track can be a single tune on an album. Tracks are assigned an order in which they appear on the album. The process of taking separate recordings of individual instruments, such as drums, bass, piano, and vocals, which have been engineered with each instrument's volume, reverb, and overall sound balanced, to create the desired "mix" for a recording.

Verse/Chorus Form: The most popular form in songwriting today. It is generally:

Verse#1, Verse#2, Chorus, Verse#3, Chorus, Bridge, Chorus.

There is a fancier form that includes a pre-chorus or "build" before each chorus.

Vignette: A particular visual moment in a story in a song, like a scene in a movie. For example, in "Jesus, Take the Wheel," when the young mother loses control of her car.

Vocable: A nonsense syllable in a song. It is always used as a hook.

Vocal chop: A heavily processed vocal or musical line that is always used as a hook.

Write to title: It means focusing your lyrics to only write about the story that is set up in your title. If you're writing "Levitating" don't talk about feeling homebound in Atlanta.

SONG LYRICS PERMISSIONS

"Better than Anything"
Lyrics by David Puretz
© 2022 David Puretz

"California"
Lyrics by Julie Logue
© 2022 Julie Logue

"Collector, The"
Lyrics by Amy Vandivort
© 2022 Amy Vandivort

"Franklin Road"
Lyrics by Jamie Parsons
© 2023 Jamie Parsons

"Here's to Life"
Music by Artie Butler
Lyrics by Phyllis Molinary
© 2023 Artie Butler and Phyllis Molinary

"He's Not Much to Look At (But He's Mine All Mine)"
Lyrics by Molly Cotten and Lilianna Wilde
© 2022 Molly Cotten and Lilianna Wilde

"How Do I Go Home Tonight?"
Lyrics by Mark Winkler and Phil Swann
© 2011 Mark Winkler and Phil Swann

"I Could Get Used to This"
Lyrics by Mark Winkler and Shelley Nyman
© 2018 Mark Winkler and Shelley Nyman

"In the Middle of the Night"
Lyrics by Mark Govatos
© 2021 Mark Govatos

"Jazz in Silhouette"
Lyrics by Mark Govatos
© 2016 Mark Govatos

"Just One"
Lyrics by Heather Perram Frank
© Heather Perram Frank

"Life After Life"
Parody Lyrics by Sue Fleg
© Sue Fleg

"Phillies 5-cent Cigars"
Lyrics by Shelley Nyman
© 2017 Shelley Nyman

"Red Toad Road"
Lyrics by Heather Perram Frank
© 2022 Heather Perram Frank

SONG LYRICS PERMISSIONS

"Rue Madame"
Parody Lyrics by Kilbourne Craddock
© 2022 Kilbourne Craddock

"Strongmen, The"
Parody Lyrics by Richard Castle
© 2022 Richard Castle

"Summer Days"
Parody Lyrics by Heather Perram Frank
© 2022 Heather Perram Frank

"Third Wheelin' at the Cracker Barrel"
Lyrics by Hannah Marie Fasick
© 2022 Hannah Marie Fasick

"Vicky Beach"
Parody Lyrics by Heather Perram Frank
© 2022 Heather Perram Frank

"You're the Top"
Parody Lyrics by Mark Govatos
© 2021 Mark Govatos

INDEX

11 o'clock number, 121
50/50 split, 199

a cappella, 172
A section, 29–30
AAAA, 60
AABA, 24, 28–30, 40, 60, 71, 99, 186
ABBA, 99
action, 209
Adele, 69, 74, 88, 164, 182
Alexander, Christel, 174
alliteration, 13, 15, 40, 71, 119, 182, 196
Amazon, 19
American Idol, 151
anaphora, 13, 71, 182, 196
Andrews Sisters, The, 89, 91
Andron, Jim, 4
Armstrong, Louis, 89, 91
ASCAP Experience, 218
assignment, 186
Associated Press, 127
At My Place, 109

Aunt Shirley, 2–4, 117
authenticity, authentic, 33, 58, 106, 180

Babyface, 19
Bacharach, Burt, 200
Bacon, Kevin, 19
Baker, John, 110
Ballantyne, Glenn, 70
Barbie, 28
Bark, 6
Bark! The Musical, 128
Bates, Stephen, 118
Beatles, 43, 46–49, 60, 131, 198
beats, 201
Beautiful, 74,
Bee Gees, 89, 92
bending words, 58
Bennett, Tony, 74
Benoit, David, 13, 165, 186, 187
Bentyne, Cheryl, 103
Bernstein, Leonard, 70
Berry, Chuck, 89, 91

Beyoncé, 11, 69
Bieber, Justin, 73
Billboard Hot 100, 16, 214
Billboard, 50, 74, 77
billboard.com, 220
Bla-Bla Café, 5
Black, Don, 41
Blanco, Benny, 214
Blocker, Don, 81
Blood, Sweat & Tears, 4
Bocelli, Andrea, 75
Bogart, Humphrey, 19
book, The, 119
Bowie, David, 89, 92
brand [v.], 15
Breakfast at Tiffany's, 35
bridge, 26, 28–29, 60, 113, 182, 208, 210, 216, 226, 228, 231
Bridgewater, Dee Dee, 6
Brighton, Barbara, 68, 189
Broadway, 41, 117
Brown, James, 89, 92
Brueggemann, Eli, 8
Bublé, Michael, 75
Butler, Artie, 137
Butler, Brett, 18

cadence, 40
Café Pacific Records, 8, 118
call and response, 72
Capricorn Rhyming Dictionary, 59
Carey, Mariah, 197
Casella, Marty, 127
Castle, Richard, 51
Catalina's, 216
Celebration Theatre, 118, 125
Celebration, The, 6
change-up, 29

character song, 132–134, 141
charm song, 121
Cheek to Cheek, 74
Cher, 174
Chicago [group], 4
chorus, 25–26, 195, 209,
Clarkson, Kelly, 182
co-writer, 114, 121, 162–166, 216, 201
Cobain, Kurt, 89, 91
Cohen, Marc, 152
Cole, Nat King, [Trio], 199–200
collaborators, 160–164
collaborators' agreement, 163,
Colonel Parker 197–198
comedy song, 121
Company I Keep, The, 36, 138
The Complete Rhyming Dictionary (Clement Wood), 59
copyright, 18, 45, 199, 201–205, 216
copyright forms, 202–205
Cotton, Molly and Wilde, Lilianna, 93
Craddock, Kilbourne, 48–49
Crawford, Randy, 6, 39
crickets, 105

David, Hal, 200
Dearie, Blossom, 61, 90
Del Belso, Richard, 126–127
DISCO.ac., 219
Douglas, Tom and Shamblin, Allen, 145
drishti, 41, 176
dummy melody, 41, 67, 208
Durango Music Festival, 218

ear candy, 40, 73
ear worms, 58
Eastern Standard Time, 61
Ebony Rain, 19, 109, 152–153

INDEX

EDM (Electronic Dance Music), 58, 74
Eminem, 57–58
end of Act One song, 120
engineer, 214

fair use, 45
Fasick, Hannah Marie, 158–59
Faust, 56
Feldshuh, Tovah, 126,
Fender Rhodes electric piano, 4
First American Records, 5, 171
Fitzgerald, Ella, 20, 55
Fleg, Sue, 52
flow, 58
folk form, 50
Footloose, 19
Forrest Gump, 73
Foster, David, 75
Frank, Heather Perram, 46–48, 83, 136
Franks, Michael, 5
Full Swing, 19
Funny Girl, 117
furniture, 36–37, 46, 48, 50, 64, 151, 174, 181, 186, 193

Gant, Dean, 39, 95
Gap Band, 88
gatekeepers, 111, 115–116, 121, 128, 210, 213
Gavotos, Mark, 146
Gay '90s Musical, The: Looking Back . . . Moving On, 118
genre, 45, 179, 182, 193, 196, 201, 215, 216, 225–229
Gentry, Bobbie, 4, 37
Gershwin, George and Gershwin, Ira, 55
Govatos, Mark, 65, 93, 84

GRAMMY[S], 50, 62, 74, 87, 137, 151
Grande, Ariana, 107, 182
Great American Songbook, 1, 7, 24, 28, 55, 73, 75, 106, 132, 190, 207–208, 225–226
Griep, Tom, 118
Groban, Josh, 75

Hadestown, 56
Hamilton, 56–57, 74
Hamilton, Arthur, 54–55
Hammerstein, II, Oscar, 69
Harris, Marilyn, 19, 36
Harrison, George, 43
Haskell, Jimmie, 4, 152
Hayes, Walker, 37
Herb Silvers band, 4
Highwaymen, The, 50
Highwomen, The, 50
Hill, Faith, 74, 134
hip hop, 24, 31, 57, 63, 69, 73, 91, 173, 179, 209, 215
Hockney, David, 82
hook[s], 13, 24, 26, 28–29, 40, 53, 58, 71–73, 135, 181, 186, 193, 195, 200, 210, 214, 226, 228, 231
Hopper, Edward, 82
Horn, Shirley, 137–138
Horne, Lena, 143
Hotel Café, 215, 219
Houston, Whitney, 197
Hozier, 20
HuffPost.com, 19
Hurder, Robyn, 125
Hyman, Rob, 18

I Can Get It for You Wholesale, 117
I want song, 120

imagery, and detail, 209
In a Lonely Place, 19
In Full Swing, 19

Jackson, Alan, 34
Jackson, Michael, 198
James, Brett, 151
Japan, 6
Jarreau, Al, 5
Jazz Life, 5, 6, 96
Jobim, Antonio Carlos, 89, 92
Joel, Billy, 4
Jordan, Brandon, 222–223
Jordan, Louis, 88, 90
Journey, 60
JustAddVocals.com, 69

K-pop, 95
Kasha, Al, 2, 40, 77, 81
KBCA, 5
KHJ "Boss Radio," 4
Kimpel, Dan, 217
King Richard, 128–129
King, Carole, 89, 92
Kinky Boots, 174
Knee Deep in Paradise, 18
Krall, Diana, 73, 90
Kramer, Matt, 109
KSDS, 108

Lady Gaga, 74
Lambert, Miranda, 182
laundry list, 28, 61–62, 64, 92, 97, 176, 182, 191, 227
Lauper, Cyndi, 18, 174
lead sheet, 201
Learning Annex, 9
Leiber and Stoller, 198

Lennon, John, 43
libretto, 119
Lindsey, Hillary, 151
Little Richard, 88,
Lizzo, 73, 89, 91
location songs, 134–135, 141
Logue, Julie, 55,135
Lorde, 28
LTD, 4
Lynn, Loretta, 89, 91
lyric sheets, 23, 216

Macklemore and Ryan, 140
Madonna, 145
Malone, Post, 15
Mancini, Henry, 35
Mandel, Johnny, 137
Manet, Edouard, 83
Manhattan Transfer, 5
Manilow, Barry, 4
Mann, Barry, 12, 30
March-Tormé, Steve, 79, 81,
Markham, Shelly, 6, 121
Marlowe, Marceline, 3
Mars, Bruno, 3, 69, 74, 87–88, 107, 131, 214
Martin, Claire, 97–98, 171
Martin, Max, 214
Mayes, Sally, 126–127
McAnally, Shane, 214
McCartney, Paul, 43, 70
McGraw, Tim, 62–63, 182
Mean Girls, 74
melismatic phrase, 41
message songs, 141
metaphor[s], 40, 196
Miles, Reid, 81
Mills, Stephanie, 4

Minnelli, Liza, 79–81, 117, 170
Minogue, Kylie, 72
Miranda, Lin-Manuel, 57, 128
Mitchell, Joni, 88, 90
Molinary, Phyllis, 137–138
money notes, 106
Montgomery, Wes, 97–98
Morrison, Barbara, 8
movie song, 159
Music Connection magazine, 217
music theory, 172
musicconnection.com, 220
musician-proof, 106

Naked Boys Singing!, 6, 7, 9, 56, 118–119, 125, 238
Nelson, Willie, 104
Netflix, 19
network (v.), 217
Networking in the Music Business, 217
New York Songwriters Circle, 220
New York Times, 18, 127
Newman, Randy, 1, 56–57, 135, 140
"Nighthawks," 82
NSAI (Nashville Songwriters Association International), 218
Nyman, Shelley, 82, 97–98, 166
Nyro, Laura, 222

Off Broadway, 6, 56
Oklahoma!, 119
open vowel, 209
opposites, 170

Page, Martin, 220
parody, 45
Parrish, Angela, 90
Parsons, Jamie, 159

payoff line, 195
People magazine, 19
Perri Sisters, 109, 110
Perry, Katy, 63
philosophy songs, 139
phrase throwing, 40
picture [songs], 151
picture title, 20, 208–210
picture words, 13, 181–182, 195, 228
Pink, 134
Play It Cool, 6,122, 123, 125–128, 155, 165
Playboy Jazz Festival, 169
poem, poetry, 40
The Police, 87
Pomeranz, David, 95
poppin', 109
"Portrait of an Artist (Pool with Two Figures)," 82
Porgy and Bess, 119
Porter, Cole, 55, 64–65, 71, 89, 92, 174, 181, 226
Poseidon Adventure, The, 2
Posner, Mike, 144
pre-chorus, 27–28, 30
Presley, Elvis, 197–198
producer, 8, 68, 75, 171, 201, 213–214, 220, 227, 231
production number, 120
prosody, 13, 40, 46, 181, 229
publisher's royalties, 198
publishing, 162, 197–201, 218
publishing agreement, 198
publishing terms, 162
Pulp Fiction, 73
Puretz, David, 64

questions, 170

R&B, 24, 58
race music, 24
Rainbow, Randy, 45
rap, 57, 58, 68, 74, 91, 173, 210–211, 229
rapper, 58
reader, 167
Realsongs, 198
Redman, Joshua, 216
Reed, Rex, 172
Reelcrafter, 219
Reeves, Dianne, 6, 13, 165, 169
refrain, 29, 71
repetition, 13, 181
return, the, 71
rewrite, 69
Rhianna, 74
rhyme scheme, 26, 29, 60
rhyme[s], rhyming, 53, 54, 57, 179, 180; double rhymes, 54, 57–58, 229; feminine rhymes, 54, 57, 229; four rhyme, 54, 230; imperfect rhyme (slant or false rhyme), 55, 59, 122, 208, 210, 229; inner rhyming/rhyme, 29, 60, 181, 230; internal rhyme, 58; masculine rhymes, 54, 57, 210; one rhymes, 54, 229; perfect rhyme, 55, 59, 119, 122, 208, 229; three rhymes, 54, 119, 229; triple rhymes, 54, 57, 229
Rich, Charlie, 20
Richard Williams, 128, 129
Robinson, Robby, 79
Rock to Recovery, 222
Rodgers and Hammerstein II, 62, 79
Rodgers, Richard and Hart, Lorenz, 55
Rosen, Sharon, 127
Russell, Brenda, 186–87

Sample, Joe, 96, 165
Sampson, Gordie, 151, 168
scansion, 25–26, 28–29, 45, 67, 181
Schrock, Bob, 6, 117–118, 121
Schwartz, Stephen, 41
Scott, Tom and the L.A. Express, 4
Shaheed, Nolan, 177
Sheeran, Ed, 3, 33, 37, 70, 89, 92, 131–132, 134, 157, 173, 210, 215
Sherwood Oaks Experimental College, 2
shout outs, 72
show, don't tell, 182, 207
Showboat, 119
Siegel, Joel E., 171
simile, 40, 196
Simon & Garfunkel, 4
Simon, John, 126
Simon, Paul, 53
Sinatra, Frank, 55, 75
singer-ese, 106
Sinne, Eeg, 68
Sondheim, Stephen, 57, 89, 91–92
songpluggers, 200
Songwriters Guild, 9, 174
Songwriting School of Los Angeles, 9
Sound of Music, The, 62
SoundCloud, 216, 219
Spears, Britney, 73
specificity, specific, 13, 33–34, 37, 46, 174
Spielberg, Steven, 151
Springsteen, Bruce, 18, 70, 107, 133, 174
Streisand, Barbra, 107, 117, 137
Sunset Boulevard, 41
Susann, Jacqueline, 18
Swann, Phil, 121–122, 124, 127, 155, 165
Swift, Taylor, 3, 33–34, 132, 135, 170

INDEX

Tales From Hollywood, 82, 171
TAXI Music, 219
TAXI Road Rally, 219
technique[s], 179
tentpole, 105
There Goes Rhymin' Simon, 53
This Side Up, 13
Till I Get It Right, 19, 105
Timberlake, Justin, 16
Tin Pan South Songwriters Festival, 218
TLC, 89, 91
"Tonight Show Starring Johnny Carson," 137
Too Old for the Chorus (But Not Too Old to be a Star!), 121–122
toplining, 69, 201, 231
Trainor, Meghan, 16, 20, 74, 170
Trotter, Jamieson, 105
Troup, Bobby, 199–200
Troup, Cynthia, 199–200
Turner, Tina, 107
Tyrell, Steve, 161, 189–191

UCLA Extension, 9
Underwood, Carrie, 73, 151

Valenzuela, Thelma, 145
Valley of the Dolls, 18
Van Zandt, Townes, 88
Vega, Suzanne, 140
verse[s], 26, 28–30, 67, 186
verse/chorus, 24–25, 27–28, 30, 40, 186

visual writer, 147
vocable[s], 26, 71–72, 196
vocal chop, 26
Vogue, 77, 78
"Voice, The," 168

Waitress, 74
Warren, Diane, 73–74, 79, 198
Webb, Jimmy, 44, 50, 52, 210
Webber, Andrew Lloyd, 41, 74
Weil, Cynthia, 12, 30
West Coast Cool, 19
Wicked, 41, 56
will.i.am and the Black-Eyed Peas, 72
Williams, Joe, 137
Williams, Pharrell, 214
Williams, Serena and Venus, 128–129
Willis, Allee, 221–222
Wilson, Brian, 88, 90
Wilson, Gretchen, 134
Winehouse, Amy, 33–34, 88
Winkler, Bob, 3
Womack, Lee Ann, 62
work for hire, 199
write to title, 179, 208
Writer Tracks, 69
writer's credit, 201
writer's royalties, 198
writer's share, 162

Yankovic, Weird Al, 45

Zepel, Arnie, 44

SONG INDEX

"99 Luftballoons," 99

"All About That Bass," 16, 20, 74

"Bali Hai," 79
"Bebop," 5
"Beguiled," 82
"Behind Closed Doors," 20
"Believe," 174
"Better Than Anything," 64
"Beyond the Sea," 98
"The Big Nowhere," (Version Two), 193
"Bridge Over Troubled Water," 4
"Bumpin'," 97–98
"Busted for Boppin'," 19
"But It Still Ain't So," 189–190

"California," 135
"Can't Get You Off of My Mind," 72
"Can't Stand the Pain," 39
"Castle on the Hill," 37
"Chasing Pavement," 74
"The Collector," 133

"Color My World," 4
"Crazy," 18
"Cry Me a River," 54–55

"Dancing in the Dark," 18
"Defying Gravity," 41
"Despacito," 99
"Diamonds," 74
"DJ Play a Christmas Song," 174
"Don't Let Me Get Me," 134
"Don't Stop Believin'," 60
"Drive (For Daddy Gene)," 34

"Ebony Rain," 109, 152–153

"Fancy Like," 37
"Fancy," 37
"Feels Like Home," 56
"Franklin Road," 159
"Future Street," 59

"Goin' Out of My Head," 4
"Gratuitous Nudity," 118

"Hard Day's Night, A," 60
"He's Not Much to Look at (But He's Mine, All Mine)," 93
"Help," 107
"Here's to Life," 137–138
"The Highwayman," 50
"The House That Built Me," 145
"How Do I Go Home Tonight?," 124

"I Could Get Used to This," 97
"I Gotta Feeling," 72
"I Hope You Dance," 62, 71
"I Took a Pill in Ibiza," 144
"Iced Frappuccinos," 21
"In My Drag," 155
"In the Middle of the Night," 93
"It's Impossible," 99

"Jazz in Silhouette," 84
"Jesus, Take the Wheel," 151
"Just Once," 12
"Just One," 83

"King Kong," 1

"Land of the Loving," 13
"Last Friday Night," 63
"Life after Life," 52
"Life Goes On," 99
"Live Like You're Dying," 62–63
"Locked Out of Heaven," 87
"Luka," 140

"Mack the Knife," 99
"Made You Look," 74
"Miss Marmelstein," 117
"Moon River," 35
"The Morning After," 2

"My Favorite Things," 62
"My Way," 99

"Night Flight," 96

"Ode to Billie Joe," 4
"On Broadway," 12
"Over the Rainbow," 28

"Papa Don't Preach,"145
"Penny Lane," 43, 45–46, 48
"Phillies 5-cent Cigars," 82
"Plum Brandy," 83

"Red Toad Road," 136
"Redneck Women," 134
"Rhode Island Is Famous for You," 61
"Robert Mitchum," 56
"(Get Your Kicks on) Route 66," 199–200
"Royals," 28
"Rue Madame," 49

"Sail Away," 140
"Same Love," 140
"Scattin' in the Moonlight," 20, 180
"SexyBack," 16
"Shake It Off," 170
"Someone Like You," 74
"Somewhere in Brazil (In the Valley)," 105
"Stay Wide Awake," 58
"The Strongmen," 51
"Summer Days," 48

"Take Me to Church," 20
"That Afternoon in Harlem," 36
"There You'll Be (Theme from Pearl Harbor)," 74

SONG INDEX

"Third Wheelin' at the Cracker Barrel," 158
"This Dance," 188
"This Side of Loving," 69
"Time after Time," 18
"Tropical Nights," 77–79, 80, 81

"Uptown Funk," 88

"Vicky Beach," 47
"Volaré," 99

"Walking in Memphis," 152
"What a Diff'rence a Day Makes," 99
"What Now My Love?," 99
"When I Was Your Man," 74
"Whiskey River," 104
"Wichita Lineman," 44

"Yesterday," 70
"You're the Top," 64–65, 71
"You've Lost That Lovin' Feelin'," 12, 30
"Your Cat Plays Piano," 147

ABOUT THE AUTHOR

Mark Winkler is a platinum award–winning singer/lyricist who has had over 250 of his songs recorded by such artists as Dianne Reeves, Liza Minnelli, Steve Tyrell, and Sara Gazarek.

His last two albums, *The Rules Don't Apply* and *Late Bloomin' Jazzman*, reached #4 and #7 on the *Jazz Week* charts, respectively, and *Late Bloomin' Jazzman* received a 4-star *DownBeat* review, as well as being awarded "Outstanding Singer/Songwriter Album" by the Bistro Awards in New York.

Winkler has performed in New York City, San Francisco, Los Angeles, London, Tokyo, and Australia.

As a lyricist, he has written six musicals including the second longest-running musical in Off-Broadway history, *Naked Boys Singing!*, which has played in New York for twenty-four years.

As an educator, Winkler has been teaching lyric writing "Crafting Great Lyrics: A Songwriters Workshop" at UCLA Extension for nineteen years and at the Los Angeles School of Songwriting for over ten years. He has started teaching his course "Lyric Writing for Jazz Singers" at Jazzvoice.com. Additionally, he writes columns for *Music Connection* magazine, *L.A. Jazz Scene*, and *Cabaret Scenes Magazine*.

He lives in Studio City, California, with his trusty yellow legal pad and his dog Stella.

www.ingramcontent.com/pod-product-compliance
Lightning Source LLC
Chambersburg PA
CBHW050347230426
43663CB00010B/2030